ISBN 978-1-330-10816-1
PIBN 10027720

1 MONTH OF
FREE
READING

at

www.ForgottenBooks.com

By purchasing this book you are eligible for one month membership to ForgottenBooks.com, giving you unlimited access to our entire collection of over 700,000 titles via our web site and mobile apps.

To claim your free month visit: www.forgottenbooks.com/free27720

Similar Books Are Available from
www.forgottenbooks.com

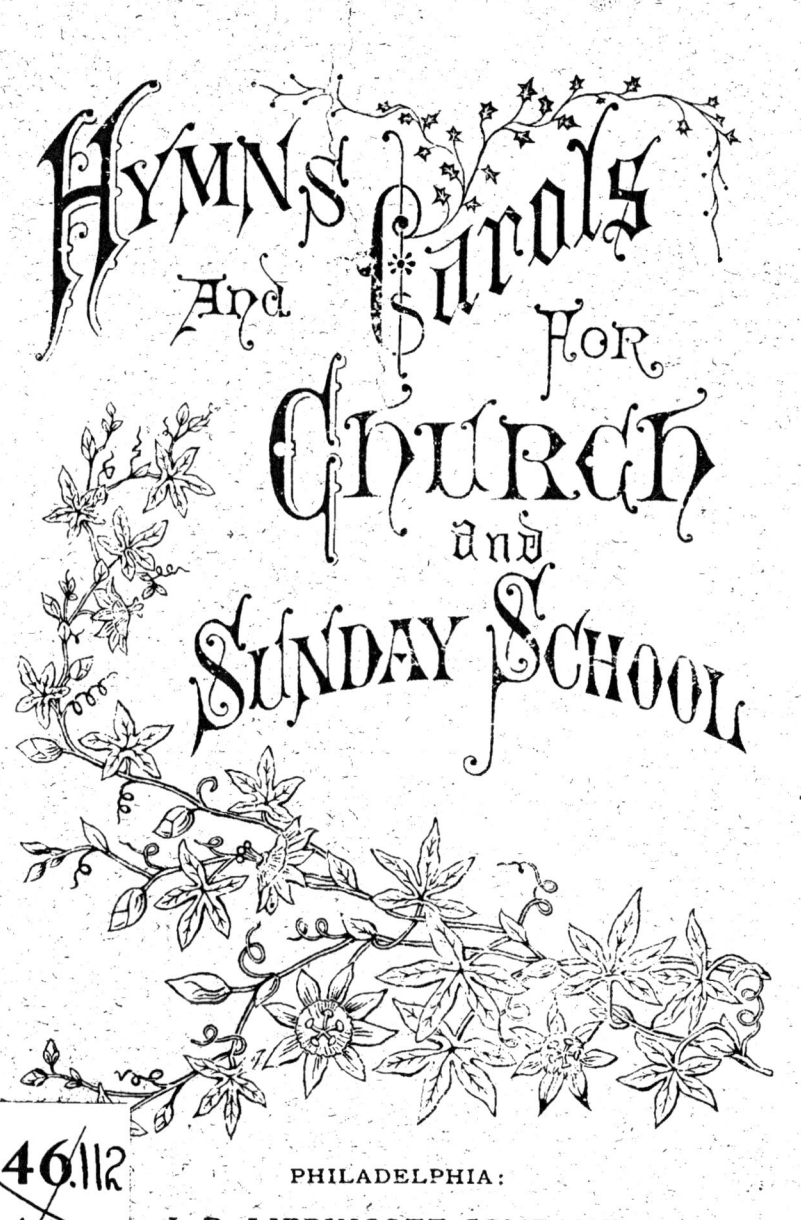

Hymns and Carols for Church and Sunday School

PHILADELPHIA:

J. B. LIPPINCOTT COMPANY.

⁕ ORDER OF WORSHIP. ⁕

9.15—DOORS CLOSED FOR PERFECT SILENCE.

OXOLOGY

Praise God, from whom all blessings flow,
Praise Him, all creatures here below;
Praise Him above, ye heavenly host,
Praise Father, Son, and Holy Ghost.

PENING HYMN.

REED—(In unison, all standing).

I believe in God the Father almighty, maker of heaven and earth; and in Jesus Christ his only Son, our Lord; which was conceived by the Holy Ghost, born of the Virgin Mary, suffered under Pontius Pilate, was crucified, dead, and buried; he descended into hell: the third day he rose again from the dead; he ascended into heaven, and sitteth on the right hand of God the Father almighty; from thence he shall come to judge the quick and the dead. I believe in the Holy Ghost; the holy catholic church; the communion of saints; the forgiveness of sins; the resurrection of the body; and the life everlasting. Amen.

RAYER HYMN.

Saviour, blessed Saviour,
  Listen while we sing,
Hearts and voices raising
  Praises to our King.
All we have to offer,
  All we hope to be,
Body, soul, and spirit—
  All we yield to Thee.

Nearer, ever nearer,
  Christ, we draw to Thee;
Deep in adoration,
  Bending low the knee.
Thou for our redemption
  Cam'st on earth to die;
Thou, that we might follow
  Hast gone up on high.

RAYER—(Repeated, all standing).

Superintendent.—God that made the world and all things therein, seeing that he is Lord of heaven and earth, dwelleth not in temples made with hands;

Secretary.   Neither is worshipped with men's hands, as though he needed any thing, seeing he giveth to all life, and breath, and all things.—Acts xvii, 24, 25.

School.—   Ye shall keep my sabbaths and reverence my sanctuary: I am the Lord.
                                                            —Lev. xix, 30

Superintendent.—God is greatly to be feared in the assembly of the saints, and to be had in reverence of all them that are about him.—Ps. lxxxix, 30.

School.—   He sent redemption unto his people; he hath commanded his covenant forever; holy and reverend is his name.—Ps. cxi, 9.

Superintendent.—And God spake all these words, saying,

School.—   I am the Lord thy God, which have brought thee out of the land of Egypt, out of the house of bondage.—Ex. xx, 1.

HYMNS AND CAROLS

FOR

CHURCH AND SUNDAY-SCHOOL.

By ALICE NEVIN.

PHILADELPHIA:
J. B. LIPPINCOTT COMPANY.

WESTCOTT & THOMSON,
Stereotypers and Electrotypers, Philada.

LIPPINCOTT'S PRESS,
Philadelphia.

PREFACE.

Hymns and Carols for Church and Sunday-School has been prepared at the request of a number of my clerical friends to meet a growing want, felt throughout many of our churches, for a more devotional and educational order of praise to be used in the service of the Sunday-school.

It is beginning to be more and more felt that the meaningless, jingling rhymes and melodies, called Sunday-school hymns and songs, with which the country is flooded, have not a formative influence upon either the moral or the religious nature of a child. Too much of the modern Sunday-school hymnology, instead of being _childlike_, is simply _childish_.

The portion of this little hymnal devoted to the older schools, generally consisting of children from ten to sixteen years of age, can be used equally well in the service of the church, as, after many years' experience in the direction of church and Sunday-school music, I have come to the conclusion that the only way to secure good congregational singing is to train up the children under a competent precentor to the use of such hymns and music as may prepare them to offer afterward an acceptable service of praise and thanksgiving in the church.

I take this opportunity of returning my sincere thanks to the many kind friends who have aided me in my work by their advice and assistance ; also to Messrs. Dutton & Co. for permission to use several of their carols.

ALICE NEVIN.

CAERNARVON PLACE, April 22, 1879.

HYMNS AND CAROLS.

Venite, Exultemus Domino.

Sir John Goss.

OH come, let us **sing** | unto · the | Lord : ‖ let us heartily **rejôice** in the | strength · of our · sal- | vation.

Let us come before His **prêsence** with | thanks- = | giving : ‖ and **show** ourselves | glad · in | Him · with | psalms.

For the **Lord** is a | great · = | God : | and a great **King** a- | bove · = | all · = | gods.

In His hand are all the **côrners** | of · the | earth : ‖ and the **strength** of the | hills · is | His · = | also.

The sea is **His,** | and · He · | made it : ‖ aud His **hands** pre- | par-ed the | dry · = | land.

Oh come, let us **wôrship,** | and · fall | down : ‖ and **kneel** be- | fore · the | Lord · our | Maker.

For **He** is the | Lord · our God : ‖ and we are the people of His **pâsture,** and the | sheep · of | His · = | hand.

Oh worship the **Lord** in the | beauty · of | holiness : ‖ let the whole **earth** | stand · in | awe · of | Him.

For He cometh, for He **cômeth** to | judge · the | earth : ‖ and with righteousness to judge the **world,** and the | peo-ple | with · His | truth.

Glory be to the **Fâther,** | and · to the | Son : ‖ **and** | to · the Ho-ly | Ghost :

As it was in the beginning, is **now,** and | ev-er | shall be : ‖ **world** | without | end. A- | MEN.

5

Gloria in Excelsis.

GREGORIAN.

Glory be to | God on | high, ‖ and on **earth** | peace, good- | will toward | men.
We praise Thee, we bless **Thee,** we | wor-ship | Thee, ‖ we glorify Thee, we give **thanks** to | Thee for | Thy great | glory.

O Lord **God,** | heavenly | King ‖ **God** the | Fa-ther | Al- — | mighty!
O Lord, the only-begotten **Son,** | Jesus | Christ, ‖ O Lord God, Lamb of **God,** | Son — | of the | Father,

That takest **away** the | sins · of the | world, ‖ have **mercy** | up-on — | us.
Thou that takest **away** the | sins · of the | world, ‖ have **mercy** | up-on — | us.
Thou that takest **away** the | sins · of the | world, ‖ re- | ceive our | prayer.
Thou that sittest at the right **hand** of | God the | Father, ‖ have **mercy** | up-on— | us.

A - MEN.

For **Thou** | only art— | holy, ‖ **Thou** | only | art the | Lord.
Thou only, O **Christ,** with the | Holy | Ghost, ‖ art most **high** in the | glory of God the Father. ‖ A— | MEN.

Gloria in Excelsis.

OLD CHANT.

GLORY be to | God · on | high : ‖ and on **earth** | peace, · good- | will · toward | men.
We praise Thee, we bless **Thee,** we | wor-ship | Thee : ‖ we glorify Thee, we give **thanks** to | Thee · for | Thy · great | glory.

O Lord **God,** | heavenly | King : ‖ **God** the | Fa-ther | Al- = | mighty.
O Lord, the only-begotten **Son,** | Je-sus | Christ : ‖ O Lord God, Lamb of **God,** | Son · = | of · the | Father,

That takest **awây** the | sins · of ͡ the | world : ‖ have **mêrcy** up- | on · = | us.
Thou that takest **awây** the | sins · of ͡ the | world : ‖ have **mêrcy** up- | on · = | us.
Thou that takest **awây** the | sins · of ͡ the | world : ‖ re- | ceive · our | prayer.
Thou that sittest at the right **hand** of | God · the | Father : ‖ have **mêrcy** up- | on · = | us.

A - MEN.

For Thou ônly | art · = | holy : ‖ **Thou** | on-ly | art · the | Lord.
Thou only, O **Christ,** with the | Ho-ly | Ghost : ‖ art most **high** in the | glory · of | God · the | Father. ‖ A- | MEN.

Te Deum Laudamus.

DEAN ALDRICH.

WE praise | Thee · O | God: ‖ we acknôwledge | Thee · to | be · the | Lord.
All the earth doth | worship | Thee: ‖ the Fâther | ev-er- | last = ing.
To Thee all angels | cry · a- | loud : ‖ the hêavens, and | all · the | powers · there- in.
To Thee, cherubim and | se-raph- | im : ‖ con- | tin-ual- | ly · do | cry;
Holy, | Ho-ly, | Holy : ‖ Lord | God · of | Sa-ba- | oth;
Hêaven and | earth · are | full : ‖ of the | majes-ty | of · Thy | glory.
The glorious company of the apôstles | praise · = | Thee : ‖
The goodly fellowship of the | pro-phets | praise · = | Thee.
The noble army of mârtyrs | praise · = | Thee : |
The holy Church throughout all the world | doth · ac- | know-ledge | Thee;
The Fâther, of an | in-finite | Majesty : ‖
Thine adôrable, | true, · and | on-ly | Son,
Alsô the | Ho-ly | Ghost : ‖
The | Com = | = · fort- | er.
Thou | art · the | King : ‖ of | glo-ry, | O = | Christ.
Thou art the ever- | last-ing | Son : ‖ of | = · the | Fa- · = ther.
When Thou tookest upon Thee to de- | liv-er | man : ‖ Thou didst humble Thysêlf to be | born · = | of · a | Virgin.
When Thou hadst overcôme the | sharpness · of | death : ‖ Thou didst open the kingdom of | heaven · to | all · be- | lievers.
Thou sittest at the right | hand · of | God : ‖ in the | glo-ry | of · the | Father.
We belîeve that | Thou · shalt | come : ‖ to | be · = | our · = | Judge.
We therefore pray Thee | help · Thy | servants : ‖ whom Thou hast redêemed | with · Thy | pre-cious | blood.
Make them to be nûmbered | with · Thy | saints : ‖ in glôry | ev-er- | last- · = | ing.
O Lord, | save · Thy | people : ‖ and | bless · Thine | her-it- | age.
Gôv- | = · ern | them : ‖ and | lift · them | up · for | ever.
Day | = · by | day : ‖ we | mag-ni- | fy = | Thee;
And we | worship · Thy | name : ‖ êver | world · with- | out = | end.
Vouch- | safe, O | Lord : ‖ to keep us | this · day | with-out | sin.
O Lord, have | mercy · up- | on us : ‖ have | mer-cy⌒up- | on · = | us.
O Lord, let Thy mêrcy | be · up- | on us : ‖ as our | trust = | is · in | Thee.
O Lord, in Thêe | have · I | trusted : ‖ let me | nev-er | be · con- | founded

Benedicite, Omnia Opera.

JAMES TUBLE.

O all ye works of the Lord, Bless ye the Lord,

praise Him, and mag - ni - fy Him for ev - er.

O ye angels of the	Lord,	bless	ye	the	Lord:
O ye	heavens,	bless	ye	the	Lord:
O ye waters that be above the	firmament,	bless	ye	the	Lord:
O all ye powers of the	Lord,	bless	ye	the	Lord:
O ye sun and	moon,	bless	ye	the	Lord:
O ye stars of	heaven,	bless	ye	the	Lord:
O ye showers and	dew,	bless	ye	the	Lord:
O ye winds of	God,	bless	ye	the	Lord:
O ye fire and	heat,	bless	ye	the	Lord:
O ye winter and	summer,	bless	ye	the	Lord:
O ye dews and	frosts,	bless	ye	the	Lord:
O ye frost and	cold,	bless	ye	the	Lord:
O ye ice and	snow,	bless	ye	the	Lord:
O ye nights and	days,	bless	ye	the	Lord:
O ye light and	darkness,	bless	ye	the	Lord:
O ye lightnings and	clouds,	bless	ye	the	Lord:
Oh let the	earth	bless	...	the	Lord: *ff* yea, let it
O ye mountains and	hills,	bless	ye	the	Lord:
O all ye green things upon the	earth,	bless	ye	the	Lord:
O ye	wells,	bless	ye	the	Lord:
O ye seas and	floods,	bless	ye	the	Lord:
O ye whales, and all that move in the	waters,	bless	ye	the	Lord:
O all ye fowls of the	air,	bless	ye	the	Lord:
O all ye beasts and	cattle,	bless	ye	the	Lord:
O ye children of	men,	bless	ye	the	Lord:
Oh let	Israel	bless	...	the	Lord:
O ye priests of the	Lord,	bless	ye	the	Lord:
O ye servants of the	Lord,	bless	ye	the	Lord:
O ye spirits and souls of the	righteous,	bless	ye	the	Lord:
O ye holy and humble men of	heart,	bless	ye	the	Lord:

Miserere Mei, Deus.

GREGORIAN.   I. 4.

HAVE = ‖ **m**ercy upon me | O God : according **to** | Thy loving-kindness.

    According unto the multitude of **Thy** | tender mercies : **blot** | out my transgressions.

    Wash me **thoroughly** | from mine iniquity : **and** | cleanse me from my sin.

    For I **acknowledge** | my transgressions : and my **sin** is | ever before me.

    Against Thee, Thee only, have I sinned, and done this evil | in Thy sight : that Thou mightest be justified when Thou speakest, **and** be | clear when Thou judgest.

    Behold I was | shapen in iniquity : and in **sin** did my | mother conceive me.

    Behold Thou desirest **truth** in the | inward parts : and in the hidden part **Thou** shalt | make me to know wisdom.

    Purge me with **hyssop**, and I | shall be clean : wash me, and I **shall** be | whi = ter than snow.

    Make me to **hear**¶ joy and gladness : that the bones which **Thou** hast | broken may rejoice.

    Hide Thy **face** | from my sins : and **blot** | out all mine iniquities.

    Create in me a **clean** | heart, O God : and renew a **right** | spirit within me.

    Cast me not **away** | from Thy presence : and take not **Thy** | Holy Spirit from me.

    Restore unto me the **joy of** | Thy salvation : and **uphold** me | with Thy free Spirit.

    Then will I teach **transgressors** | Thy ways : and sinners shall **be con-** | verted unto Thee.

    Deliver me from blood-guiltiness, O God, Thou **God** of | my salvation : and my tongue shall sing **aloud** | of Thy righteousness.

    O **Lord,** open | Thou my lips : and my mouth **shall** | show forth Thy praise.

    For Thou desirest not sacrifice, else | would I give it : Thou **delight**est | not in burnt offerings.

    The sacrifices of **God** are a | broken spirit : a broken and a contrite heart, O **God,** Thou wilt not despise.

    Do go**o**d in Thy good **pleasure** | unto Zion : build Thou the **walls of Jerusa**-em.

    Then shalt Thou be pleased with the sacrifices of righteousness, with burnt **offering,** and | whole burnt offering : then shall they **offer** bullocks | upon Thine altar.

Glo-ry ‖ be to the **Father** and to the Son : **and** | to the Holy Ghost ;

As it ‖ was in the beginning, is **now,** and | ever shall be : **world** | without end. AMEN.

Deus Misereatur.

GREGORIAN.   VIII. 2.   *Rouen Mediation.*

God · be ‖ **mêrciful** unto | us, · and · bless · us : and show us the light of His countenance **and** be | merci-ful · un-to · *us ;*

That Thy **way** may be | known · upon · *earth* : Thy saving **health** a- | *mong* · *all* · na-tions.

Let the people **praise** | Thee, · O · *God* : yea, let **all** the | peo-ple · *praise* · *Thee.*

Oh let the nations **rejôice,** | and · be · *glad* : for Thou shalt judge the folk right-eously, and **gôvern** the | na-tions⌒up-*on* · *earth.*

Let the people **praise** | Thee, · O · *God* : yea, let **all** the | peo-ple · *praise* · *Thee.*

Then shall the **earth** bring | forth · her · in-crease : and God, even our own **God,** shall | give · us · *His* · bless-ing.

God shall | *bless · us* : and all the ends of the | world · shall · *fear · Him.*

Glo-ry | be to the **Fâther** | and · to · the⌒*Son* : **and** | to · the · Ho-ly · *Ghost ;*

As · it ‖ was in the beginning, is **now,** and | ev-er · shall   be   **world** with- | out end.   Ā-men.

Gloria Patri.

GREGORIAN.   VII. 4.

Glo-ry ‖ be to the **Fâther,** | and · to · the ⌒*Son* : **and** | to · the · Ho-ly · Ghost;

As it ‖ was in the beginning, is **now,** and | ev-er · shall · be : **world** with- | out end.   A-men.

Benedic, Anima Mea.

ANCIENT THEME.

PRAISE the **Lord,** | O · my | soul : ‖ and all that is **within** me | praise · His | holy | name.
Praise the **Lord,** | O · my | soul : ‖ and forget **not** | all · His | ben-e- | fits;
Who **forgiveth** | all · thy | sin : ‖ and healeth all | thine · in- | firm-i- | ties;
Who saveth thy **life** | from · de | struction : ‖ and crowneth thee with **mercy** and | lov-ing- |
     kind- = | ness.
Oh praise the Lord, ye angels of His, ye that ex- | cel · in | strength : ‖ ye that fulfill His com-
     mandment, and **hearken** unto the | voice · of | His · = | word.
Oh praise the **Lord,** all | ye · His | hosts : ‖ ye **servants** of | His that | do · His | pleasure.
Oh speak good of the Lord, all ye works of His, in all **places** of | His do- | minion : | praise
     thou the **Lord,** | O · = | my · = | soul.
Glory be to the **Father,** | and · to the | Son : ‖ **and** | to · the | Holy | Ghost;
As it was in the beginning, is **now,** and | ev-er | shall be : ‖ **world** | without | end. A- | MEN.

Jubilate Deo.

GREGORIAN.   VI. 2.

OH · be ‖ joyful in the **Lord** | all · ye · lands : serve the Lord with gladness, and come **before**
     His | pre-sence · with · a · song.
     Be ye sure that the **Lord,** | He · is · God : ‖ it is He that hath made us, and not we
         ourselves ; we are His people, and the **sheep** | of · His · *pas*-ture.
     Oh go your way into His gates with thanksgiving, and **into** His | courts · with ·
         praise : be thankful unto **Him,** and | speak · good · of · His name.
     For the Lord is gracious, His **mercy** is | ev-er-lasting : and His truth endureth from
         generation to | gen-er-*a*-tion.
Glo-ry ‖ be to the **Father,** | and · to · the Son : **and** | to · the · Ho-ly · Ghost;
As it was in the beginning, is **now,** and | ev-er | shall be : ‖ **world** | without | end. A- | MEN.

Magnificat.

Sir John Goss.

My soul doth **mâgni-** | fy ˙ the | Lord : ‖ and my spirit **hath** re- | joiced ˙ in | God ˙ my Saviour.
For He | hath ˙ re- | garded : ‖ the low **estate** | of ˙ His | hand- = | maiden.
For be- | hold, ˙ from | henceforth : ‖ **all gener-** | ations ˙ shall | call ˙ me | blessed.
For He that is mighty hath **done to** | me great | things : ‖ **and** | ho-ly | is ˙ His name.
And His mercy is on **them** that | fear ˙ = | Him : ‖ **from generation** | to— | gen-er- | ation.
He hath showed **strength** | with ˙ His | arm : ‖ He hath scattered the **proud** in the imagin- | a-tion | of ˙ their | hearts.
He hath put down the **mighty** | from ˙ their | seat : ‖ and **hath** exalted | them of | low de- | gree.
He hath filled the **hûngry** | with ˙ good | things : ‖ and the **rich** He | hath ˙ sent | empty ˙ a- | way.
He remembering His mercy hath holpen His **sêrvant** | Is-ra- | el : ‖ as He promised to our forefathers, **Abraham** | and ˙ his | seed, ˙ for ever.
Glory be to the **Fâther,** | and ˙ to the | Son : ‖ **and** | to ˙ the | Ho-ly | Ghost;
As it was in the beginning, is **now,** and | ev-er | shall be : ‖ **world** with- | out ˙ end.
A- = men.

Nunc Dimittis.

Rev. W. Felton.

Lord, now lettest Thou Thy **sêrvant** de- | part ˙ in | peace : ‖ **ac-** | cording | to ˙ Thy | word.
For mine | eyes ˙ have | seen : ‖ **Thy** | sal- = | va- = | tion,
Which **Thou** | hast ˙ pre-pared : ‖ **befôre** the | face ˙ of | all ˙ = | people ;
To be a **light** to | lighten ˙ the | Gentiles : ‖ and to be the **glôry** of Thy | peo-ple | Is-ra- | el.
Glory be to the **Fâther,** | and ˙ to the | Son : ‖ **and** | to ˙ the | Ho-ly | Ghost;
As it was in the beginning, is **now,** and | ev-er | shall be : ‖ **world** | without | end. A- | men.

Benedictus.

I. ROBINSON.

BLESSED be the Lord **God** of | Is-ra- | el : ‖ for He hath vísited | and · re- | deemed · His | people;
And hath raised up a mighty salvâtion | for · = | us : ‖ in the **house** | of · His | ser-vant | David;
As He spake by the **mouth** of His | ho-ly | prophets : ‖ which have **been** | since · the | world · be- | gan;
That we should be sâved | from · our | enemies : ‖ and from the **hand** of | all · that | hate · = | us:
Glory be to the **Fâther,** | and · to the | Son : ‖ **and** | to · the | Ho-ly | Ghost;
As it was in the beginning, is **now,** and | ev-er | shall be : ‖ **world** | without | end. A- | MEN.

The Lord's Prayer.

OUR Father who art in **heaven,** | hallowed | be Thy | name ‖ Thy kingdom come, Thy will be **dcne,** on | earth as it | is in | heaven.
Give us th is | day our | daily | bread ‖ and forgive us our **debts** as | we for- | give our | debtors,
And lead us not into **temptation,** but de- | liver | us from | evil, | for Thine is the kingdom, and the power, and the **glory** for | ever. | A- — | MEN.

Bonum Est Confiteri.

I. TURLE.

It is a good thing to give **thanks** | unto · the | Lord : ‖ and to sing praises unto Thy **name,**
  O · = | Most · = | Highest.
To tell of Thy loving-kindness **êarly** | in · the | morning : ‖ and of Thy **truth** | in · the
  night · = | season.
Upon an instrument of ten **strings,** and up- | on · the | lute : ‖ upon a loud **instrument,**
  and · up- | on · the | harp.
For Thou, Lord, hast made me **glad** | through · Thy | works : ‖ and I will rejoice in giving
  praise for the oper- | a-tions | of · Thy | hands.
Glo-ry be to the **Fâther,** | and · to the | Son : | **and** | to · the | Ho-ly | Ghost;
As it was in the beginning, is **now,** and | ev-er | shall be : ‖ **world** | without end. A- | MEN.

The Lord's Prayer.

GREGORIAN.   TONUS REGIUS.

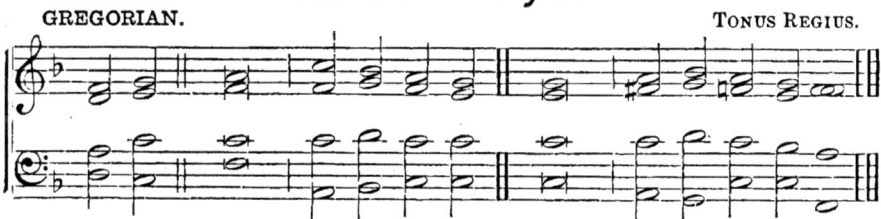

Our | Father who art in heaven, **hallowed** | be Thy name, | Thy kingdom come, Thy will
  be **done** on | earth as it is in heaven;
  Give us this **day** our | daily bread | and forgive us our **debts** as | we forgive our
  debtors.
  And lead us not into temptation, but **deliver** | us from evil | for Thine is the kingdom,
  and the power, and the **glory,** for | ever. A- —MEN.

Seraphic Hymn.

HOWARD.

Ho - ly, ho - ly, ho - ly Lord God of Sa - ba - oth; Heaven and earth are

full, are full of the ma - jes - ty of Thy glo - ry. Ho - san - na, Ho -

san - na, Ho - san - na in the highest! Blessed is He that com - eth in the

name of the Lord. Ho - san - na, Ho - san - na, Ho - san - na in the high - est!

1   *Lo, He Comes, with Clouds Descending.*

ST. THOMAS. 8s, 7s & 4.   V. NOVELLO.

1. Lo, He comes, with clouds descend-ing, Once for favored sin - ners slain;

Thousand thousand saints at - tend-ing Swell the triumph of His train :

Al - le - lu - ia! Al - le - lu - ia! Christ the Lord re - turns to reign. A-MEN.

2 Every eye shall now behold Him
  Robed in dreadful majesty ;
Those who set at naught and sold Him,
  Pierced, and nail'd Him to the tree,
    Deeply wailing,
Shall the true Messiah see.

3 Every island, sea and mountain,
  Heaven and earth, shall flee away ;
All who hate Him must, confounded,
  Hear the trump proclaim the day ;
    Come to judgment,
Come to judgment, come away.

4 Now redemption, long expected,
  See in solemn pomp appear
All His saints, by men rejected,
  Now shall meet Him in the air.
    Alleluia!
See the day of God appear.

5 Yea, Amen! let all adore Thee,
  High on Thine eternal throne ;
Saviour, take the power and glory,
  Claim the kingdom for Thine own.
    Oh come quickly,
  Alleluia! Come, Lord, come. AMEN.

Charles Wesley and John Pennick. Altered by M. Maden.

2

2   *Rejoice, all ye Believers.*

MUNICH. 7s & 6s. D.   GERMAN MELODY.

1. { Re - joice, all ye be - liev-ers! And let your lights ap - pear; }
{ The eve - ning is ad - vanc -ing, And dark - er night is near. }

The Bridegroom is a - ris - ing, And soon He draw - eth nigh;

Up! pray, and watch, and wres - tle; At midnight comes the cry. A-MEN.

2 The watchers on the mountain
   Proclaim the Bridegroom near;
Go meet Him, as He cometh,
   With hallelujahs clear;
The marriage-feast is waiting,
   The gates wide open stand;
Up! up! ye heirs of glory!
   The Bridegroom is at hand.

3 Ye saints who here in patience
   Your cross and sufferings bore
Shall live and reign for ever
   Where sorrow is no more;

Around the throne of glory
   The Lamb ye shall behold,
In triumph cast before Him
   Your diadems of gold.

4 Our Hope and Expectation,
   O Jesus! now appear;
Arise, thou Sun so longed for,
   O'er this benighted sphere:
With hearts and hands uplifted,
   We plead, O Lord! to see
The day of earth's redemption,
   That brings us unto Thee. AMEN.

Laurentius Laurenti, 1700.   Trans. Jane Borthwick, 1853

3   *Hosanna to the Living Lord.*

HOSANNA. **L. M.** (With Chorus.)   Rev. Dr. DYKES.

1. Ho - san - na to the liv - ing Lord! Ho - san - na to th'in - car - nate Word!

To Christ, Cre - a - tor, Sa-viour, King, Let earth, let heav'n, Ho - san - na sing.

Ho - san - na, Lord! Ho - san - na in the high - est!   A - MEN.

2 Hosanna, Lord! Thine angels cry;
  Hosanna, Lord! Thy saints reply;
  Above, beneath us, and around,
  The dead and living swell the sound:
Hosanna, Lord! Hosanna in the highest!

3 O Saviour, with protecting care,
  Return to this Thy house of prayer;
  Assembled in Thy sacred name,
  Where we Thy parting promise claim.
Hosanna, Lord! Hosanna in the highest!

4 But, chiefest in our cleansèd breast,
  Eternal bid Thy Spirit rest,
  And make our secret soul to be
  A temple pure, and worthy Thee.
Hosanna, Lord! Hosanna in the highest!

5 So in the last and dreadful day,
  When earth and heaven shall melt away,
  Thy flock, redeemed from sinful stain,
  Shall swell the sound of praise again:
Hosanna, Lord! Hosanna in the highest!
           AMEN.
          Reginald Heber.

4   *Come, Kingdom of our God.*

CARLISLE. S. M.   C. LOCKHART.

1. Come, kingdom of our God, Sweet reign of life and love; Shed
peace and hope and joy a - broad, And wis - dom from a - bove. A-MEN.

2 Over our spirits first
   Extend thy healing reign;
Then raise and quench the sacred thirst
   That never pains again.

3 Come, kingdom of our God,
   And make the broad earth thine;
Stretch o'er her land and isles the rod
   That flowers with grace divine.

4 Soon may all tribes be blest
   With fruit from life's glad tree,
And in its shade like brothers rest,
   Sons of one family.

5 Come, kingdom of our God,
   And raise thy glorious throne
In worlds by the undying trod,
   When God shall bless His own. AMEN
              Johns (Lyr. Amer., 1865).

5   *Hail! Thou long-expected Jesus.*

SAXONY. 8s & 7s.   G. K. OLIVER.

1. Hail! Thou long-ex-pect-ed Je-sus, Born to set Thy peo-ple free;

SAXONY.—Continued.

From our fears and sins release us; Let us find our rest in Thee. A - MEN.

2 Israel's strength and consolation,
   Hope of all the earth Thou art;
Long desired of every nation,
   Joy of every waiting heart.

3 Born Thy people to deliver,
   Born a child, yet God our King,

Born to reign in us for ever,
   Now Thy gracious kingdom bring.
4 By Thine own eternal Spirit
   Rule in all our hearts alone;
   By Thine all-sufficient merit
   Raise us to Thy glorious throne. AMEN.
                              Charles Wesley, 1744.

6   *Lift up the Advent Strain.*

Sir JOHN GOSS.

1. Lift up the ad - vent strain! Be - hold, the Lord is nigh!

Greet His approach, ye saints, a-gain, With hymns of ho - ly joy. A - MEN.

2 Daughter of Sion, rise
   To meet thy lowly King;
Nor let the faithless heart despise
   The peace He comes to bring.

3 As Judge in clouds of light
   He shall come down again,
And all His scattered saints unite
   With Him in heaven to reign. AMEN.

7   *O'er the Distant Mountains Breaking.*

SALZBURG.   8s, 7s & 4.   MICHAEL HAYDN.

1. O'er the dis-tant mountains breaking, Comes the red'ning dawn of day:

Rise, my soul, from sleep a - wak-ing, Rise and sing, and watch and pray:

'Tis thy Sa-viour, 'Tis thy Saviour, On His bright re - turn - ing way.   A-MEN.

2 O Thou long-expected, weary
　　Waits my anxious soul for Thee;
Life is dark and earth is dreary,
　　Where Thy light I do not see;
　　　　O my Saviour,
　　When wilt Thou return to me?

3 Long, too long in sin and sadness,
　　Far away from Thee, I pine,
When, oh when, shall I the gladness
　　Of Thy Spirit feel in mine?
　　　　O my Saviour,
　　When shall I be wholly Thine?

4 Nearer is my soul's salvation,
　　Spent the night, the day at hand;
Keep me in my lonely station,
　　Watching for Thee, till I stand,
　　　　O my Saviour,
　　In Thy bright and promised land.

5 With my lamp well trimmed and burn-
　　　ing,
　　Swift to hear and slow to roam,
Watching for Thy glad returning
　　To restore me to my home;
　　　　Come, my Saviour,
　　O my Saviour, quickly come! AMEN
　　　　　　　　　J. S. B. Monsell.

8 *Hark, the Glad Sound! the Saviour Comes.*

CHOPIN. C. M.   ANON.

1. Hark, the glad sound! the Saviour comes, The Saviour prom - is'd long;

Let ev' - ry heart pre-pare a throne, And ev' - ry voice a song,

And ev - 'ry voice a song. A - MEN.

2 On Him the Spirit, largely pour'd,
　Exerts its sacred fire;
Wisdom and might, and zeal and love,
　His holy breast inspire.

3 He comes the pris'ners to release
　In Satan's bondage held;
The gates of brass before Him burst,
　The iron fetters yield.

4 He comes from thickest films of vice
　To clear the mental ray,

And on the eyeballs of the blind
　To pour celestial day.

5 He comes the broken heart to bind,
　The bleeding soul to cure,
And with His righteousness and grace
　T' enrich the humble poor.

6 Our glad hosannas, Prince of peace,
　Thy welcome shall proclaim,
And heav'n's eternal arches ring
　With Thy beloved name. AMEN.

Philip Doddridge.

9   *Watchman, Tell us of the Night.*

WATCHMAN. 7s.   Dr. L. Mason.

1. Watchman, tell us of the night, What its signs of prom-ise are.

Traveler, o'er you mountain's height See that glo - ry-beam-ing star.

Watchman, does its beauteous ray Aught of hope or joy fore - tell?

Traveler, yes; it brings the day— Promised day of Is - ra - el.

CHORUS to 1st and 2d stanzas.

Traveler, yes; it brings the day— Promised day of Is - ra - el.

CHORUS to 3d stanza.

Traveler! lo! the Prince of peace, Lo! the

Son of God is come, Lo! the Son of God is come.

2 Watchman, tell us of the night;
  Higher yet that star ascends.
Traveler, blessedness and light,
  Peace and truth, its course portends.
Watchman, will its beams alone
  Gild the spot that gave them birth?
Traveler, ages are its own;
  See, it bursts all o'er the earth.

3 Watchman, tell us of the night,
  For the morning seems to dawn.
Traveler, darkness takes its flight;
  Doubt and terror are withdrawn.
Watchman, let thy wanderings cease;
  Hie thee to thy quiet home;
Traveler, lo! the Prince of peace,
  Lo! the Son of God, is come!

Sir John Bowring (1825).

10   *Jesus, Thy Church with Longing Eyes.*

DUKE STREET. L. M.   H. HATTON.

1. Je - sus, Thy Church with long - ing eyes For thine ex - pect - ed com - ing waits. When will the prom - ised light a - rise, And glo - ry beam from Zi - on's gates? A - MEN.

2 Oh come and reign o'er every land;
  Let Satan from his throne be hurled,
All nations bow to Thy command,
  And grace receive a dying world.

3 Teach us, in watchfulness and prayer,
  To wait for the appointed hour,
And fit us, by Thy grace, to share
  The triumphs of Thy conq'ring power.
AMEN.

Wm. H. Bathurst.

11   *Come Hither, Ye Faithful.*

PORTUGUESE HYMN. 11s.   Arr. by P. READING.

1. Come hith - er, ye faith - ful; tri - umph-ant - ly sing: Come
see in the man-ger the an - gels' dread King! To Beth - le - hem
hast - en with joy - ful ac - cord; Oh come ye, come hither, Oh
come ye, come hither, Oh come ye, come hither, to worship the Lord. A-MEN.

2 True Son of the Father, He comes from the skies;
To be born of a virgin He does not despise;

To Bethlehem hasten, with joyful accord;
‖:Oh come ye, come hither,:‖ to worship the Lord!

3 Hark, hark to the angels, all singing
  in heaven,
  "To God in the highest all glory be
  given!"
  To Bethlehem hasten with joyful accord;
  ‖: Oh come ye, come hither, :‖ to worship
  the Lord!

4 To Thee, then, O Jesus, this day of Thy
  birth,
  Be glory and honor through heaven
  and earth,
  True Godhead incarnate! omnipotent
  Word!
  ‖: Oh come, let us hasten : ‖ to worship the
  Lord! AMEN.

  Latin Hymn. Fifteenth Century.

12 *Joy to the World!*

ANTIOCH. C. M.   Arr. by LOWELL MASON.

1. Joy to the world! the Lord is come! Let earth re-ceive her King; Let
ev'-ry heart pre-pare Him room, And heav'n and nature sing, And
And heav'n and nature
heav'n and nature sing, And heav'n, and heav'n and na-ture sing. A-MEN.
sing,
And heav'n and nature sing.

2 Joy to the earth! the Saviour reigns!
  Let men their songs employ,
  While fields and floods, rocks, hills and
  plains,
  Repeat the sounding joy.

3 No more let sins and sorrows grow,
  Nor thorns infest the ground;
  He comes to make His blessings flow
  Far as the curse is found.

  Isaac Watts, 1709.

13   *Hark! the Herald Angels Sing.*

MENDELSSOHN. 7s.   MENDELSSOHN.

1. Hark! the her - ald au - gels sing,   "Glo - ry to   the   new - born King;

Peace on earth and mer - cy   mild,   God and sin - ners rec - on - ciled!

Joy - ful, all ye   na - tions, rise,   Join the triumph of   the   skies;

With th'an-gel - ic   host pro-claim Christ is   born   in Beth - le - hem!"

MENDELSSOHN.—Continued.

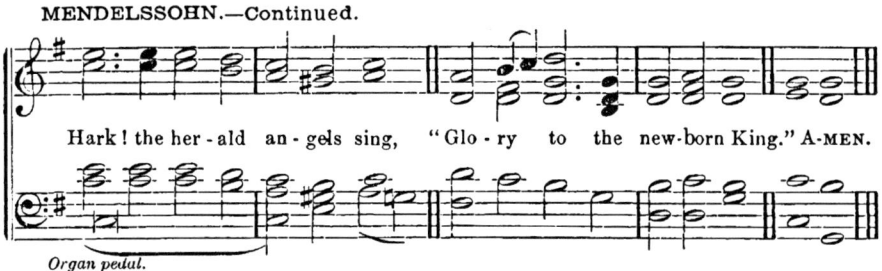

Hark! the her-ald an-gels sing, "Glo-ry to the new-born King." A-men.

Organ pedal.

2 Hail, the heavenly Prince of peace!
Hail, the Sun of righteousness!
Light and life to all He brings,
Risen with healing in His wings.

Mild, He lays His glory by,
Born that man no more may die,
Born to raise the sons of earth,
Born to give them second birth.
Hark! etc. AMEN.

Charles Wesley.

14   *Hark! what Mean those Holy Voices.*

HOLY VOICES. 8s & 7s.

1. Hark! what mean those ho-ly voi-ces, Sweet-ly sound-ing through the skies?

Lo! th'angel-ic host re-joi-ces, Heav'nly hal-le-lu-jahs rise. A-MEN.

2 Listen to the wondrous story,
  Which they chant in hymns of joy:
"Glory in the highest, glory!
  Glory be to God most high!

3 "Peace on earth, good-will from heaven,
  Reaching far as man is found;
Souls redeemed, and sins forgiven,
  Loud our golden harps shall sound.

4 "Christ is born, the great Anointed;
  Heaven and earth His praises sing!
Oh, receive whom God appointed
  For your Prophet, Priest, and King.

5 "Hasten, mortals, to adore Him;
  Learn His name and taste His joy,
Till in heaven ye sing before Him,
  'Glory be to God most high!'" AMEN.

John Cawood, 1825.

15   *All my Heart this Night Rejoices.*

Rev. ANGELO A. BENSON. (Trans. 1862.)   J. G. EBELING (1620–1672), 1666.

1. All my heart this night re - joi - ces, As I hear, Far and near,

Sweetest an - gel voi - ces. "Christ is born!" their choirs are sing - ing,

Till the air Ev - 'ry - where Now with joy is ring - ing.

2 Hark! a voice from yonder manger,
     Soft and sweet,
     Doth entreat,
" Flee from woe and danger;
Brethren, come; from all doth grieve you
     You are freed;
     All you need
I will surely give you."

3 Come, then, let us hasten yonder;
     Here let all,
     Great and small,
Kneel in awe and wonder.

Love Him who with love is yearning;
     Hail the star
     That from far
Bright with hope is burning!

4 Ye who pine in weary sadness,
     Weep no more,
     For the door
Now is found of gladness.
Cling to Him, for He will guide you
     Where no cross,
     Pain or loss,
Can again betide you.

16   *The Lowly Crib in Bethlehem's Stall.*

Arr. from HANDEL.

1. The low - ly crib in Bethl' - hem's stall, The
Child of won - der, All in All! Glo - ry to God,
Glo - ry to God, Glo - ry to God in the high - est!

2 " Proud Israel's Hope, the world's Desire!"
So sang of old the angelic choir.
    Glory to God, etc.

3 "On earth sweet peace, to men goodwill;
Let joy the distant nations fill."
    Glory to God, etc.

4 Let children's voices, clear and strong,
The Christ-child's glories still prolong.
    Glory to God, etc.

5 From far and near the pine-branch bring
And crown the cradle of our King.
    Glory to God, etc.

6 Messiah, Jesu, Babe divine,
Unceasing praises still be Thine.
    Glory to God, etc.

7 Let heaven and earth with praises ring;
Blest Trinity, to Thee we sing:
    Glory to God, etc.

Edwin A. Gernaut.

17   *Hark! a Burst of Heavenly Music.*

Words by Mrs. M. N. MEIGS.   Music by FRED. SCHILLING.

1. Hark! a burst of heavenly mu - sic From a band of ser - aphs bright,

Sud - den - ly to earth descend - ing, In the calm and si - lent night:

To the shepherds of Ju - de - a, Watching in the earl - iest dawn,

So they bear the joy - ful tidings, "Je - sus, Prince of peace, is born."

HARK! A BURST OF HEAVENLY MUSIC.—Continued.

CHORUS.

Sweet and clear those an - gel voi - ces, Echoing thro' the storm - y sky,

As they chant the heavenly mu - sic, "Glo - ry be to God on high!"

2 Slumbering in a lowly manger
  Lies the mighty Lord of all,
And before the holy Stranger
  See the trembling shepherds fall.
He has come, the long-expected,
  Full of wisdom, love, and grace,
To redeem His ruined creatures,
  To restore our fallen race.

Cho.—So let angels wake the chorus,
  So let ransomed men reply,
Chanting the celestial anthem,
  "Glory be to God on high!"

3 And this joyful Christmas morning,
  Breaking o'er the world below,
Tells again the wondrous story
  Shepherds heard so long ago.
Who shall still our tuneful voices,
  Who the tide of praise shall stem,
Which the blessed angels taught us
  In the fields of Bethlehem?

Cho.—Hark! we hear again the chorus
  Ringing through the starry sky,
And we join the heavenly anthem,
  "Glory be to God on high!"

18   *What Child is This ?*

Poetry by W. C. DIX.   Old English.

1. What child is this, who, laid to rest, On Ma-ry's lap is sleep-ing? Whom

2

WHAT CHILD IS THIS?—Continued.

An - gels greet with an- thems sweet, While shepherds watch are keep - ing?

ff *CHORUS.*

This, this is Christ the King, Whom shepherds guard and an - gels sing:

Haste, haste to bring Him laud, The Babe, the Son of Ma - ry.

2 Why lies He in such mean estate,
　　Where ox and ass are feeding?
Good Christian, fear; for sinners here
　　The silent Word is pleading;
Nails, spear, shall pierce Him through,
　　The cross be borne for me, for you;
Hail, hail, the Word made flesh,
　　The Babe, the Son of Mary.

3 So bring Him incense, gold, and myrrh,
　　Come peasant, king, to own Him:
The King of kings salvation brings,
　　Let loving hearts enthrone Him.
Raise, raise, the song on high,
　　The Virgin sings her lullaby;
Joy, joy, for Christ is born,
　　The Babe, the Son of Mary

19   *A Shepherd Band.*

PRÆTORIUS, 1609.

1. A shepherd band their flocks are keeping, And gen - tle lambs are sweet - ly sleeping, When sud-den-ly they all be - hold An an - gel in bright robes, with harp . . . . of gold.

2 Glad tidings of great joy he bringeth,
The azure vault with anthems ringeth;
"Immanuel" awakes the song,
And countless hosts the glorious theme prolong.

3 "To you, this day, is born a Saviour,
Your Prophet, Priest, and King for ever.
All glory be to God!" they cry;
"All glory be to God!" let earth reply.

4 The shepherds view the host returning,
Their hearts with holy ardor burning;
To Bethlehem they wend their way,
Repeating with glad tongues th' angelic lay.

5 In haste they seek the heavenly Stranger;
They find the Babe laid in a manger;
With wonder and with awe they fall,
And joyfully adore Him, Lord of all.

6 Now every voice with rapture swelleth,
For Christ the Lord with mortals dwelleth;
Let men and angels Him adore,
And shout their loud hosannahs evermore.

20   *Carol, Carol, Christians.*

1. Car - ol, car - ol, Chris-tians, Car - ol joy - ful - ly,
D.C. Car - ol, car - ol, Chris-tians, Car - ol joy - ful - ly,

Car - ol for the com - ing Of Christ's na - tiv - i - ty;
Car - ol for the com - ing Of Christ's na - tiv - i - ty.

And pray a gladsome Christmas For all good Christian men. Car- ol, car- ol,

Chris - tians, Christmas come a - gain. Car- ol, car- ol,

2 Go ye to the forest,
　Where the myrtles grow,
Where the pine and laurel
　Bend beneath the snow,
And gather them for Jesus,
　Wreathe them for His shrine,
Make His temple glorious
　With the box and pine.
　　Carol, carol,
　　　Carol, carol, Christians,
　　Carol joyfully,
　　　Carol for the coming
　　Of Christ's nativity.

3 Give us grace, O Saviour,
　To put off in might
Deeds and dreams of darkness
　For the robes of light,
That we may live as lowly
　As Thyself with men,
So to rise in glory
　When Thou comest again.
　　Carol, carol,
　　　Carol, carol, Christians,
　　Carol joyfully,
　　　Carol for the coming
　　Of Christ's nativity.

21   *Christ is Born of Maiden Fair.*

Dr. GAUNTLETT.

1. Christ is born of mai-den fair; Hark! the her-alds in the air Thus a-
dor-ing des-cant there: "In ex-cel-sis glo - - ri-a."

2 Shepherds saw those angels bright,
　Caroling in glorious light;
　"God, His Son is born to-night,
　　In excelsis gloria."

3 Christ is come to save mankind,
　As in holy page we find,
　Therefore this song bear in mind,
　　"*In excelsis gloria.*"

22   Angels, from the Realms of Glory.

Music by W. B. GILBERT.

1. An - gels, from the realms of glo - - ry   Wing your flight o'er

all   the earth; Ye who sang cre - a - tion's sto - - ry,

Now pro - claim Mes - si - ah's birth. Come and wor - ship,

Come and wor - ship,   Wor - ship Christ, the new - born King! A - MEN.

2 Shepherds in the field abiding,
    Watching o'er your flocks by night,
God with man is now residing:
    Yonder shines the infant-light.
        Come and worship,
    Worship Christ, the new-born King.

3 Saints before the altar bending,
    Watching long in hope and fear,
Suddenly the Lord, descending,
    In His temple shall appear.
        Come and worship,
    Worship Christ, the new-born King.
        AMEN.

By permission of E. P. Dutton & Co.

23 The Virgin's Cradle-Song.

JOSEPH BARNBY.

1. The Vir-gin stills the cry-ing Of Je-sus, sleepless ly-ing; And

sing-ing for His plea-sure, Thus calls u-pon her trea-

sure: "My darl-ing, do not weep, My Je-sus, sweet-ly sleep."

2 "O Lamb, my love inviting.
O Star, my soul delighting,
O Flower of mine own bearing,
O Jewel past comparing!
        My darling, etc.

3 "My Child of might indwelling,
My Sweet, all sweets excelling,

Of bliss the Fountain flowing,
The Day-spring ever glowing.
        My darling, etc.

4 "My joy, my exultation,
My spirit's consolation,
My Son, my Spouse, my Brother,
Oh listen to thy mother!
        My darling," etc.

24 In Excelsis Gloria.

Music by ED. T. POTTER.

1. When Christ was born of Ma - ry free, In Beth'lem, in that fair cit - y,

An - gels sang with mirth and glee, In ex - cel - sis glo - ri - a!

CHORUS.

cres. *rall.*

In ex - cel - sis glo - ri - a! In ex - cel - sis glo - ri - a! In ex - cel - sis,

In ex - cel - sis, In ex - cel - sis glo - ri - a!

2 Herdsmen beheld these angels bright,
To them appearing with great light,
Who said, God's Son is born this night,
In excelsis gloria!

3 This King is come to save mankind,
As in Scripture truths we find,

Therefore this song have we in mind,
In excelsis gloria!

4 Therefore, Lord, for Thy great grace
Grant us the bliss to see Thy face;
There we shall sing to Thy solace,
In excelsis gloria!

By permission of E. P. Dutton & Co.

25   *All this Night Bright Angels Sing.*

ARTHUR S. SULLIVAN.

1. All this night bright angels sing; Nev-er was such car - ol-ing. Hark! a voice which loud - ly cries, "Mortals, mor-tals, wake and rise. Lo! to glad-ness Turns your sad - ness: From the earth is ris'n a Sun Shines all night tho' day be done."

2 Wake, O earth, wake everything,
Wake and hear the joy I bring:
Wake and joy, for all this night
Heaven and every twinkling light,
All amazing,
Still stand gazing,
Angels, powers, and all that be,
Wake, and joy this Sun to see.

3 Hail! O Sun, O blessed Light,
Sent into this world by night;
Let Thy rays and heavenly powers
Shine in these dark souls of ours,
For most duly
Thou art truly
God and man, we do confess;
Hail, O Sun of righteousness!

26 *See Amid the Winter's Snow.*

Sir JOHN GOSS.

SOLO. (*Treble or Tenor alternately.*)

1. See a - mid the win - ter's snow, Born for us on earth below,

Mod.

See the ten - der Lamb ap-pears, Prom-ised from e - ter - nal years.

CHORUS. *ff*

Hail! thou ev - er - bless - ed morn! Hail! re-demp-tion's hap - py dawn!

SEE AMID THE WINTER'S SNOW.—Continued.

Sing through all Je - ru - sa - lem, Christ is born in Beth - le - hem.

2 Lo! within a manger lies
He who built the starry skies,
He who, throned in height sublime,
Sits amid the cherubim.—Cho.

3 Say, ye holy Shepherds, say,
What your joyful news to-day;
Wherefore have ye left your sheep
On the lonely mountain steep?—Cho.

4 "As we watched at dead of night,
Lo! we saw a wondrous light;
Angels singing ' Peace on earth !'
Told us of the Saviour's birth."—Cho.

5 Sacred Infant, all divine,
What a tender love was Thine,
Thus to come from highest bliss
Down to such a world as this!—Cho.

27 *A Babe is Born in Bethlehem.* Old English.

1. A Babe is born in Beth - le- hem, Therefore re-joice, Je - ru - sa -lem.

Hal - le - lu - jah, Hal - le - lu - jah, Hal - le - lu - jah, A - men.

2 Within a manger He doth lie
Whose throne is set above the sky.
Hallelujah, etc.

3 Stillness was all the manger round,
The creature its Creator found.

4 Our human flesh He enters in,
But bears no single taint of sin.

5 To fallen man Himself He bowed,
That He might lift us up to God.

6 On this most blessed jubilee
All glory be, O God, to Thee.

7 O holy Three, we Thee adore,
This day, henceforth, for evermore.
Hallelujah, etc. AMEN.

28　　*Good News from Heaven the Angels Bring.*

C. STEGGALL, Mus. Doc.

1. Good news from heav'n the angels bring, Glad tidings to the earth they sing: To us this day a Child is giv'n, To crown us with the joy of heav'n. Al-le-lu-ia, Al-le-lu-ia, Al-le-lu-ia, Al-le-lu-ia, Al-le-lu-ia, Al-le-lu-ia.

2　This is the Christ, our God and Lord,
　Who in all need shall aid afford;
　He will Himself our Saviour be,
　From all our sins to set us free.

3　All hail, Thou noble Guest, this morn,
　Whose love did not the sinner scorn;
　In my distress Thou comest to me:
　What thanks shall I return to Thee?

4　Were earth a thousand times as fair,
　Beset with gold and jewels rare,

She yet were far too poor to be
A narrow cradle, Lord, for Thee.

5　Ah, dearest Jesus, holy Child,
　Make Thee a bed, soft, undefiled,
　Within my heart, that it may be
　A quiet chamber kept for Thee.

6　Praise God upon His heavenly throne,
　Who gave to us His only Son;
　For this His hosts, on joyful wing,
　A blest New Year of mercy sing.

29 *For Thy Mercy and Thy Grace.*

HORTON. 7s.   SCHNYDER VON WARTENSEE.

1. For Thy mer - cy and Thy grace, Faith - ful through an-
oth - er year, Hear our song of thank - ful - ness,
Fa - ther and Re - deem - er, hear. A - MEN.

2 In our weakness and distress,
    Rock of strength! be Thou our
      stay;
  In the pathless wilderness
  Be our true and living way.

3 Who of us death's awful road
    In the coming year shall tread,
  With Thy rod and staff, O God,
  Comfort Thou his dying head.

4 Keep us faithful, keep us pure,
    Keep us evermore Thine own;
  Help, oh help us to endure,
  Fit us for Thy promised crown.

5 So within Thy palace gate
    We shall praise, on golden strings,
  Thee, the only Potentate,
  Lord of lords and King of kings.
                  AMEN.
          Henry Downton, 1843.

30　Great God! We Sing that Mighty Hand.

MENDON. L. M.　　　　　　　　　　　　　　　　　GERMAN.

1. Great God! we sing that might-y Hand By which sup-port-ed still we stand: The opening year Thy mer-cy shows; Let mer-cy crown it till it close. A-MEN.

2　By day, by night, at home, abroad,
　Still we are guarded by our God;
　By His incessant bounty fed,
　By His unerring counsel led.

3　With grateful hearts the past we own;
　The future, all to us unknown,
　We to Thy guardian care commit,
　And, peaceful, leave before Thy feet.

4　In scenes exalted or deprest,
　Be Thou our joy, and Thou our rest;
　Thy goodness all our hopes shall raise,
　Adored through all our changing days.

5　When death shall interrupt our songs,
　And seal in silence mortal tongues,
　Our helper, God, in whom we trust,
　In better worlds our soul shall boast.
　　　　　　　　　　　　　　AMEN.

31   *Hail to the Lord's Anointed.*

HOLY DAYS.   7s & 6s. D.   F. WEBER.

1. Hail to the Lord's a - noint-ed, Great Da - vid's great-er Son! }
See in the time ap - point-ed His reign on earth be gun! }

He comes to break op - pres - sion, To set the cap - tive free,

To take a - way trans-gres - sion, To rule in eq - ui - ty. A - MEN.

2 Before Him on the mountains
  Shall Peace, the herald, go,
And from a thousand fountains
  Shall grace unceasing flow;
Kings shall fall down before Him,
  And gold and incense bring;
All nations shall adore Him,
  His praise all people sing.

3 To Him shall prayer unceasing
  And daily vows ascend,
His kingdom still increasing—
  A kingdom without end.
O'er every foe victorious,
  He on His throne shall rest,
From age to age more glorious,
  All-blessing and all-blest. AMEN.
        James Montgomery, 1822.

32   *As with Gladness Men of Old.*

DIX. 7s.   CONRAD KOCKER.

1. As with gladness men of old   Did the guiding star behold,   As with joy they hailed its light,   Leading on-ward, beaming bright,   So, most gra - cious Lord, may we   Ev - er - more be led to Thee.   A - MEN.

2 As with joyful steps they sped
  To that lowly manger-bed,
  There to bend the knee before
  Him whom heaven and earth adore,
  So may we with willing feet
  Ever seek the mercy-seat.

3 As they offered gifts most rare
  At that manger rude and bare,
  So may we with holy joy,
  Pure and free from sin's alloy,
  All our costliest treasures bring,
  Christ, to Thee, our heavenly King.

4 Holy Jesu, every day
  Keep us in the narrow way,
  And when earthly things are past
  Bring our ransomed souls at last
  Where they need no star to guide,
  Where no clouds Thy glory hide.

5 In the heavenly country bright
  Need they no created light,
  Thou its Light, its Joy, its Crown,
  Thou its Sun which goes not down,
  There for ever may we sing
  Alleluias to our King. AMEN.

W. C. Dix, 1860.

33   *Jesus shall Reign where'er the Sun.*

MEDWAY. L. M.   PERGOLESI.

1. Je - sus shall reign wher - e'er the sun Does his suc - cess - ive jour - neys run; His king - dom stretch from shore to shore, Till moons shall wax and wane no more. A - MEN.

2 To Him shall endless prayer be made,
And praises throng to crown His head;
His name like sweet perfume shall rise
With every morning sacrifice.

3 People and realms of every tongue
Dwell on His love with sweetest song,
And infant voices shall proclaim
Their early blessings on His name.

4 Blessings abound where'er He reigns,
The prisoner leaps to burst his chains,
The weary find eternal rest,
And all the sons of want are blest.

5 Let every creature rise and bring
Peculiar honors to our King;
Angels descend with songs again,
And earth repeat the loud Amen.
                 AMEN.
               Isaac Watts.

4

34　　*Christ, whose Glory fills the Skies.*

DAY-SPRING.　7s.　　　　　　　　　　PRUSSIAN AIR.

1. Christ, whose glo - ry fills the skies, Christ, the true, the on - ly Light,

Sun of right - eous-ness, a - rise, Tri - umph o'er the shades of night;

Day-spring from on high, draw near; Day-star, in our hearts ap-pear. A-MEN.

2 Dark and cheerless is the morn
　Unaccompanied by Thee,
Joyless is the day's return,
　Till Thy mercy's beams we see;
Lord, Thy inward light impart,
Cheering each benighted heart.

3 Visit every soul of Thine,
　Pierce the gloom of sin and grief;
Fill with radiancy divine,
　Scatter all our unbelief;
More and more Thyself display,
Shining to the perfect day. AMEN.

Charles Wesley, 1740

35 *Love Divine, all Loves Excelling.*

OTTO. 8s & 7s.

1. Love di - vine, all loves ex - cel - ling, Joy of heaven to earth come down, }
Fix in us Thy hum - ble dwell-ing; All Thy faith - ful mercies crown: }

Je - sus, Thou art all com - pas - sion, Pure un - bound-ed love Thou art;

Vis - it us with Thy sal - va-tion; En - ter ev'-ry trembling heart. A-MEN.

2 Breathe, oh breathe Thy loving Spirit
  Into every troubled breast,
Let us all in Thee inherit,
  Let us find the promised rest;
Take away our power of sinning,
  Alpha and Omega be;
End of faith, as its beginning,
  Set our hearts at liberty.

3 Come, almighty to deliver,
  Let us all Thy life receive,
Suddenly return, and never,
  Never more Thy temples leave;

Thee we would be always blessing,
  Serve Thee as Thy hosts above,
Pray, and praise Thee without ceasing,
  Glory in Thy perfect love.

4 Finish, then, Thy new creation,
  Pure and sinless let us be;
Let us see Thy great salvation
  Perfectly restored in Thee,
Changed from glory into glory,
  Till in heaven we take our place,
Till we cast our crowns before Thee,
  Lost in wonder, love, and praise.

           AMEN.

Charles Wesley, 1746.

36 *We Three Kings of Orient are.*

SOLI.

1. We three kings of O- ri- ent are; Bear-ing gifts, we traverse a - far.

Field and foun - tain, moor and mountain, Following yon - der Star.

CHORUS.

O Star of wonder, Star of night, Star with roy - al beau- ty bright,

West-ward lead - ing, Still pro - ceed - ing, Guide us to Thy per - fect light.

2 Born a King on Bethlehem plain,
    Gold I bring to crown Him again;
        King for ever,
        Ceasing never,
    Over us all to reign.
                O Star, etc.

3 Frankincense to offer have I
    Incense owns a Deity nigh;
        Prayer and praising
        All men raising,
    Worship Him, God on high.
                O Star, etc.

4 Myrrh is mine; its bitter perfume
    Breathes a life of gathering gloom;
        Sorrowing, sighing,
        Bleeding, dying,
    Sealed in the stone-cold tomb.
                O Star, etc.

5 Glorious now behold Him arise,
    King and God and Sacrifice;
        Heaven sings
        "Hallelujah!"
    "Hallelujah!" the earth replies.
                O Star, etc.

37   *O Jesus, God and Man.*

BOYLSTON. S. M.   LOWELL MASON.

1. O Je - sus, God and Man, On this Thy ho - ly day

To Thee for pre - cious gifts of grace Thy ransomed peo - ple pray. A - MEN.

2 We pray for childlike hearts,
    For gentle, holy love,
For strength to do Thy will below
    As angels do above.

3 We pray for simple faith,
    For hope that never faints,
For true communion evermore
    With all Thy blessed saints.

4 On friends around us here
    Oh let Thy blessing fall;
We pray for grace to love them well,
    But Thee beyond them all.

5 Oh joy to live for Thee!
    Oh joy in Thee to die!
Oh very joy of joys to see
    Thy face eternally! AMEN!
                Sir Henry W. Baker, 1852.

38 *Alleluia, Songs of Sweetness.*

REGENT SQUARE. 8s & 7s.   HENRY SMART.

1. Al - le - lu - ia, songs of sweetness, Voice of joy that can - not die,

Al - le - lu - ia is the anthem Ev - er dear to choirs on high;

In the house of God a - bid - ing, Thus they sing e - ter - nal - ly. A-MEN.

2 Alleluia, thou resoundest
    True Jerusalem and free;
Alleluia, joyful mother,
    All thy children sing with thee;
But by Babylon's sad waters
    Mourning exiles now are we.

3 Alleluia cannot always
    Be our song while here below;
Alleluia, our transgressions
    Make us for a while forego;

For the solemn time is coming
When our tears for sin must flow.

4 Therefore in our hymns we pray Thee,
    Grant us, blessed Trinity,
At the last to keep Thine Easter
In our home beyond the sky,
There to Thee for ever singing
Alleluia joyfully. AMEN.

Adam St. Victor.
Trans. by J. M. Neale. Altered

39 *Brightest and Best of the Sons of the Morning.*

WESLEY. 11s & 10s.

LOWELL MASON.

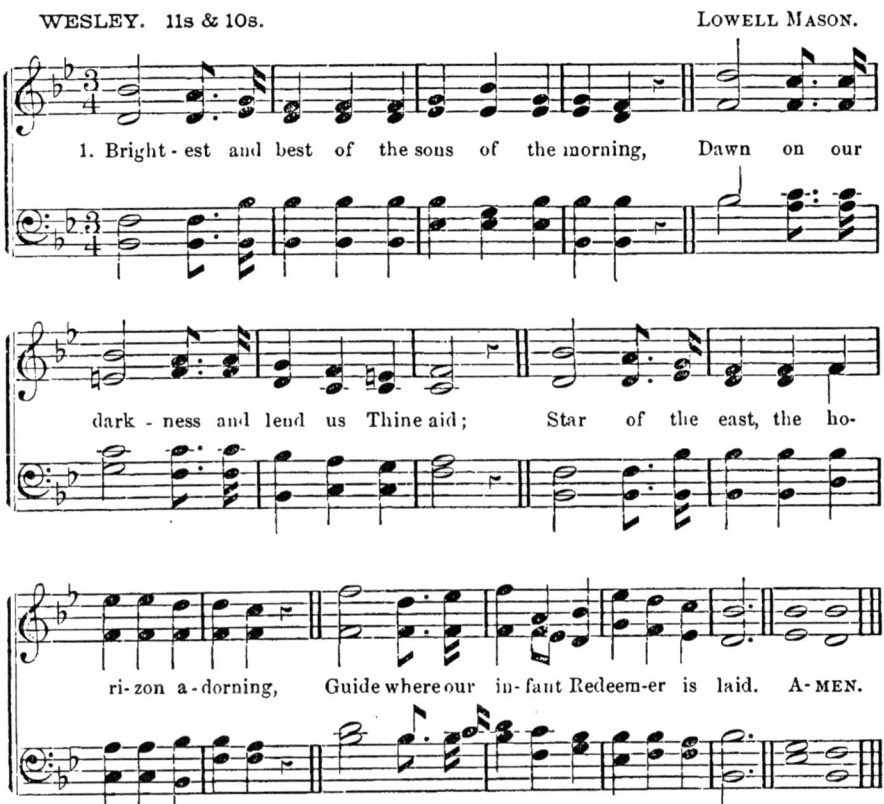

1. Bright-est and best of the sons of the morning, Dawn on our dark-ness and lend us Thine aid; Star of the east, the ho-ri-zon a-dorning, Guide where our in-fant Redeem-er is laid. A-MEN.

2 Cold on His cradle the dewdrops are shining,
  Low lies His head with the beasts of the stall;
  Angels adore Him in slumber reclining,
  Maker and Monarch and Saviour of all.

3 Say, shall we yield Him, in costly devotion,
  Odors of Edom and offerings divine,
  Gems of the mountain and pearls of the ocean,
  Myrrh from the forest, and gold from the mine?

4 Vainly we offer each ample oblation,
  Vainly with gifts would His favor secure;
  Richer by far is the heart's adoration,
  Dearer to God are the prayers of the poor.

5 Brightest and best of the sons of the morning,
  Dawn on our darkness and lend us Thine aid;
  Star of the East, the horizon adorning,
  Guide where our infant Redeemer is laid. AMEN.

Reginald Heber, 1411.

40 *The Star in the East.*

Rev. W. H. Cooke.

1. In the win-try hea - ven Shines a wondrous star, ... In the East the wise men Watch it from a - far, Ask-ing, "What this lus - tre, So un-earth-ly bright?" Answering, "Christ in glory Comes to earth to-night."

2 O'er the dusty highways,
   O'er the deserts drear,
From the East, the wise men
   Watch it shining clear,
Asking, "Shall we follow
   In this starlit way?"
Answering, "Yes, 'twill lead us
   To the perfect day."

3 In a lowly manger
   Lies an Infant weak :
Is it He whom wise men
   Come so far to seek?

Asking, "Where the Monarch?
   Where Judæa's King?"
Saying, "Gifts and worship
   To His throne we bring."

4 In our hearts we children
   See this star once more—
Not as wise men saw it
   In the days of yore—
Asking, "May we bring Him
   Childish love to-day?"
Answering, "Come, dear children ;
   Jesus says we may."

41   *Jesus, Lover of my Soul.*

MARTYN. 7s. D.   L. B. MARSH.

1. Je - sus, Lov - er of my soul, Let me to Thy bos - om fly, ⎫
While the near - er wa - ters roll, While the tem - pest still is high; ⎭

{ Hide me, O my Sa - viour, hide, ⎫
{ Till the storm of life is past; ⎭ Safe in - to the

ha - ven guide; Oh, re-ceive my soul at last. A - MEN.

2 Other refuge have I none,
   Hangs my helpless soul on Thee;
Leave, ah, leave me not alone,
   Still support and comfort me;
All my trust on Thee is stayed,
   All my help from Thee I bring;
Cover my defenceless head
   With the shadow of Thy wing.

3 Thou, O Christ, art all I want—
   More than all in Thee I find;
Raise the fallen, cheer the faint,
   Heal the sick, and lead the blind;

Just and holy is Thy name,
   I am all unrighteousness;
False and full of sin I am,
   Thou art full of truth and grace.

4 Plenteous grace with Thee is found,
   Grace to cover all my sin;
Let the healing streams abound,
   Make and keep me pure within.
Thou of life the Fountain art,
   Freely let me take of Thee,
Spring Thou up within my heart,
   Rise to all eternity. AMEN.

Charles Wesley, 1740.

42   *My Sins, my Sins, my Saviour!*

AURELIA.   7s & 6s.   Dr. S. S. WESLEY.

1. My sins, my sins, my Sa - viour! They take such hold on me

I am not a - ble to look up, Save on - ly, Christ, to Thee:

In Thee is all for - give-ness, In Thee a - bun - dant grace,

My shad-ow and my sun-shine The brightness of Thy face. A-MEN.

2 My sins, my sins, my Saviour!
  How sad on Thee they fall
Seen through Thy gentle patience,
  I tenfold feel them all.
I know they are forgiven,
  But still their pain to me
Is all the grief and anguish
  They laid, my Lord, on Thee.

3 My sins, my sins, my Saviour!
  Their guilt I never knew
Till with Thee in the desert
  I near Thy passion drew,

Till with Thee in the garden
  I heard Thy pleading prayer,
And saw the sweat-drops bloody
  That told Thy sorrow there.

4 Therefore my songs, my Saviour
  E'en in this time of woe,
Shall tell of all Thy goodness
  To suffering man below—
Thy goodness and Thy favor,
  Whose presence from above
Rejoice those hearts, my Saviour,
  That live in Thee, and love. AMEN.
J. S. B. Monsell, 1863.

43   *Saviour, when in Dust to Thee.*

SPANISH HYMN. 7s. D.   SPANISH MELODY.

1. Sa - viour, when in dust to Thee Low we bend th'a - dor - ing knee,
When, re-pent - ant, to the skies Scarce we lift our weep - ing eyes,—

D.C. Bending from Thy throne on high, Hear our sol - emn Lit - a - ny.

Oh, by all Thy pains and woe, Suffered once for man be - low, A-MEN.

2 By Thy helpless infant years,
By Thy life of want and tears,
By Thy days of sore distress
In the savage wilderness,
By the dread, mysterious hour
Of th' insulting tempter's power,
Turn, oh turn a favoring eye,
Hear our solemn Litany.

3 By Thine hour of dire despair,
By Thine agony of prayer,
By the cross, the nail, the thorn,
Piercing spear and torturing scorn,

By the gloom that veiled the skies
O'er the dreadful sacrifice,
Listen to our humble cry,
Hear our solemn Litany.

4 By Thy deep expiring groan,
By the sad sepulchral stone,
By the vault whose dark abode
Held in vain the rising God,—
Oh, from earth to heaven restored,
Mighty, reascended Lord,
Listen, listen to the cry
Of our solemn Litany. AMEN.
Robert Grant, 1815.

44   *Nearer, my God, to Thee.*

BETHANY.   6s & 4s.   LOWELL MASON.

1. Near-er, my God, to Thee, Near-er to Thee, E'en though it be a cross

That rais-eth me; Still all my song shall be, Near-er, my God, to Thee,

Near - er, my God, to Thee, Near - er to Thee.. A - MEN.

2 Though, like the wanderer,
  The sun gone down,
Darkness be over me,
  My rest a stone,
Yet in my dreams I'd be
Nearer, my God, to Thee,
  Nearer to thee.

3 There let my way appear,
  Steps unto heaven;
All that Thou sendest me
  In mercy given;
Angels to beckon me
Nearer, my God, to Thee,
  Nearer to Thee.

4 Then, with my waking thoughts
  Bright with Thy praise,
Out of my stony griefs
  Bethel I'll raise;
So by my woes to be
Nearer, my God, to Thee,
  Nearer to Thee.

5 Or if on joyful wing
  Cleaving the sky,
Sun, moon, and stars forgot,
  Upward I fly,
Still all my song shall be,
Nearer, my God, to Thee,
  Nearer to Thee. AMEN.

Sarah L. Adams, 1848.

45   *Second Tune.*

KEDRON. 6s & 4s.   A. B. SPRATT.

Near - er, my God, to Thee, Near - er to Thee, E'en though it
be a cross That rais - eth me; Still all my song shall be,
Near - er, my God, to Thee, Near - er to Thee. A - MEN.

46　　　*Rock of Ages, Cleft for Me.*

TOPLADY. 7s. 6 lines.　　　　　　　　　THEO. HASTINGS.

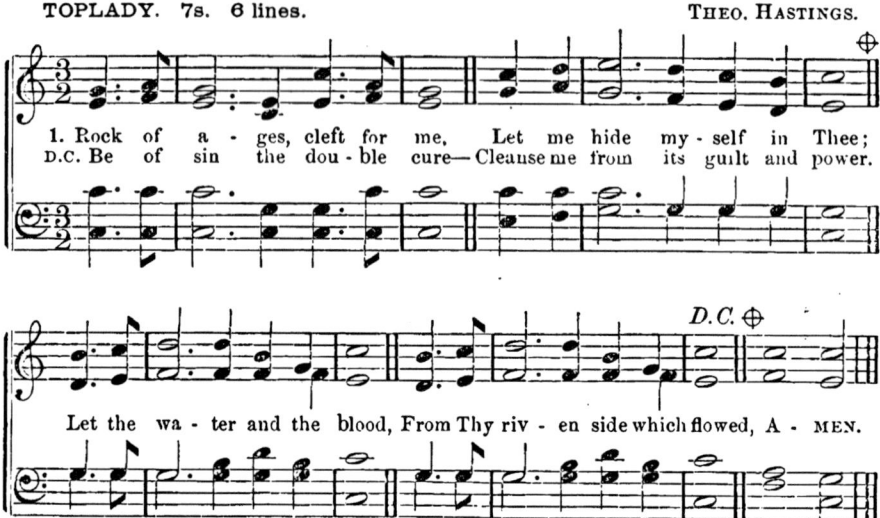

1. Rock of a - ges, cleft for me, Let me hide my - self in Thee;
D.C. Be of sin the dou - ble cure—Cleanse me from its guilt and power.

D.C.

Let the wa - ter and the blood, From Thy riv - en side which flowed, A - MEN.

2 Not the labors of my hands
　Can fulfill Thy law's demands;
　Could my zeal no respite know,
　Could my tears for ever flow,
　All for sin could not atone:
　Thou must save, and Thou alone.

3 Nothing in my hand I bring,
　Simply to Thy cross I cling;
　Naked, come to Thee for dress,
　Helpless, look to Thee for grace;

Foul, I to the fountain fly;
Wash me, Saviour, or I die.

4 While I draw this fleeting breath,
　When my eyelids close in death,
　When I soar to worlds unknown,
　See Thee on Thy judgment-throne,
　Rock of ages, cleft for me,
　Let me hide myself in Thee. AMEN.

Augustus M. Toplady, 1776.

47　·　*O Thou from whom all Goodness flows.*

MANOAH. C. M.　　　　　　　　　From G. ROSSINI.

1. O Thou from whom all goodness flows, I lift my heart to Thee;

MANOAH.—Continued.

In all my sorrows, conflicts, woes, O Lord, re-mem-ber me. A-MEN.

2 When, with a broken, contrite heart,
　I lift mine eyes to Thee,
Thy name proclaim, Thyself impart,
　In love remember me.

3 In sore temptations, when no way
　To shun the ill I see,

My strength proportion to my day,
　And then remember me.

4 And when I tread the vale of death,
　And bow at Thy decree,
Then, Saviour, with my latest breath
　I'll cry, "Remember me." AMEN.

Thomas Haweis, 1792.

48　*Dear Father, to Thy Mercy-seat.*

ARLINGTON.　C. M.　　　　　　　　　　　　　　　　F. A. ARNE.

1. Dear Father, to Thy mer-cy-seat My soul for shel-ter flies;

'Tis here I find a safe re-treat When storms and tempests rise. A - MEN.

2 My cheerful hope can never die
　If Thou, my God, art near ;
Thy grace can raise my comforts high
　And banish every fear.

3 My great Protector and my Lord,
　Thy constant aid impart ;

Oh, let Thy kind, Thy gracious word
　Sustain my trembling heart !

4 Oh, never let my soul remove
　From this divine retreat ;
Still let me trust Thy power and love,
　And dwell beneath Thy feet. AMEN.

Anne Steele.

49   *There is a Fountain filled with Blood.*

WOODLAND.   C. M.   N. D. GOULD.

1. There is a foun - tain filled with blood Drawn from Im - man - uel's veins,

And sin - ners plunged be - neath that flood, And sin - ners plunged be-

neath that flood, Lose all their guilt - y stains. A - MEN.

2 The dying thief rejoiced to see
    That fountain in his day,
‖: And there have I, as vile as he, :‖
    Washed all my sins away.

3 Dear, dying Lamb, Thy precious blood
    Shall never lose its power
‖: Till all the ransomed Church of God : ‖
    Be saved to sin no more.

4 E'er since, by faith, I saw the stream
    Thy flowing wounds supply,
‖: Redeeming love has been my theme, : ‖
    And shall be till I die.

5 Then, in a nobler, sweeter song,
    I'll sing Thy power to save
‖: When this poor, lisping, stamm'ring
    tongue : ‖
    Lies silent in the grave.   AMEN.
                     William Cowper, 1779.

50   *Just as I am, Without one Plea.*

ST. CRISPIN. 8s.   Sir G. F. ELVEY.

1. Just as I am, with - out one plea, But that Thy blood was

shed for me, And that Thou bidd'st me come to Thee,

O Lamb of God, I come, I come. A - MEN.

2 Just as I am, and waiting not
  To rid my soul of one dark blot,
  To Thee, whose blood can cleanse each
      spot,
    O Lamb of God, I come, I come.

3 Just as I am, though tossed about
  With many a conflict, many a doubt,
  Fightings and fears within, without,
    O Lamb of God, I come, I come.

4 Just as I am, poor, wretched, blind,
  Sight, riches, healing of the mind—

  Yea, all I need—in Thee to find,
    O Lamb of God, I come, I come.

5 Just as I am Thou wilt receive,
  Wilt welcome, pardon, cleanse, relieve;
  Because thy promise I believe,
    O Lamb of God, I come, I come

6 Just as I am, Thy love unknown
  Has broken every barrier down;
  Now to be Thine—yea, Thine alone—
    O Lamb of God, I come, I come.
               AMEN.
         Charlotte Elliott, 1836.

5

51   *Lord, in this Thy Mercy's Day.*

ST. PHILIP.   7s. 3 lines.   W. H. MONK.

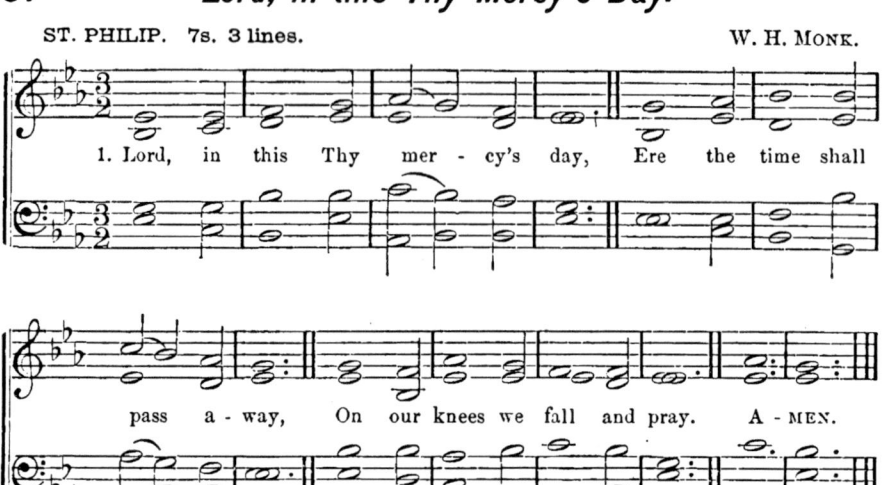

1. Lord, in this Thy mer - cy's day, Ere the time shall pass a - way, On our knees we fall and pray. A - MEN.

2 Holy Jesus, grant us tears,
Fill us with heart-searching fears,
Ere the hour of doom appears.

3 Lord, on us Thy Spirit pour,
Kneeling lowly at Thy door,
Ere it close for evermore.

4 By Thy night of agony,
By Thy supplicating cry,
By Thy willingness to die,

5 By Thy tears of bitter woe
For Jerusalem below,—
Let us not Thy love forego.

6 Judge and Saviour of our race,
When we see Thee face to face,
Grant us 'neath Thy wings a place.

7 On Thy love we rest alone,
And that love will then be known
By the pardoned 'round Thy throne.
AMEN.
Rev. I. Williams, 1841.

52   *Not all the Blood of Beasts.*

ST. THOMAS.   S. M.   I. WILLIAMS.

1. Not all the blood of beasts On Jew - ish al - tars slain Could

ST. THOMAS.—Continued.

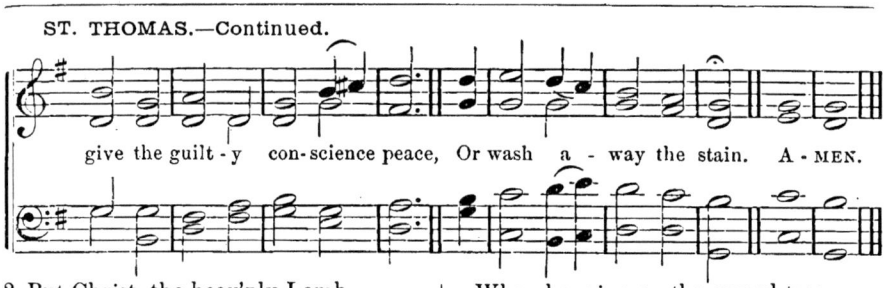

give the guilt-y con-science peace, Or wash a - way the stain. A - MEN.

2 But Christ, the heav'nly Lamb
  Takes all our sins away,
  A Sacrifice of nobler name
  And richer blood than they.

3 My soul looks back to see
  The burdens Thou didst bear

When hanging on the cursed tree,
  And hopes her guilt was there.

4 Believing, we rejoice
  To see the curse remove;
  We bless the Lamb with cheerful voice,
  And sing His bleeding love. AMEN.
  Isaac Watts, 1709.

53   *Sweet the Moments, Rich in Blessing.*

ST. AUGUSTINE.   8s & 7s.   BACH. (Arr. A. N.)

1. Sweet the moments, rich in blessing, Which be - fore the cross I spend,

Life and health and peace possessing From the sinner's dying Friend. A - MEN.

2 Truly blessed is the station
  Low before His cross to lie,
  While I see divine compassion
  Floating in His languid eye.

3 Here it is I find my heaven,
  While upon the Lamb I gaze;

Love I much? I've much forgiven;
  I'm a miracle of grace

4 Love and grief my heart dividing,
  With my tears His feet I'll bathe;
  Constant still in faith abiding,
  Life deriving from His death. AMEN.
  James Allen, 1757. Altered by Walter Shirley, 1776.

54   *Art thou Weary, art thou Languid?*

STEPHANOS.   8s, 5, & 3.   W. H. MONK.

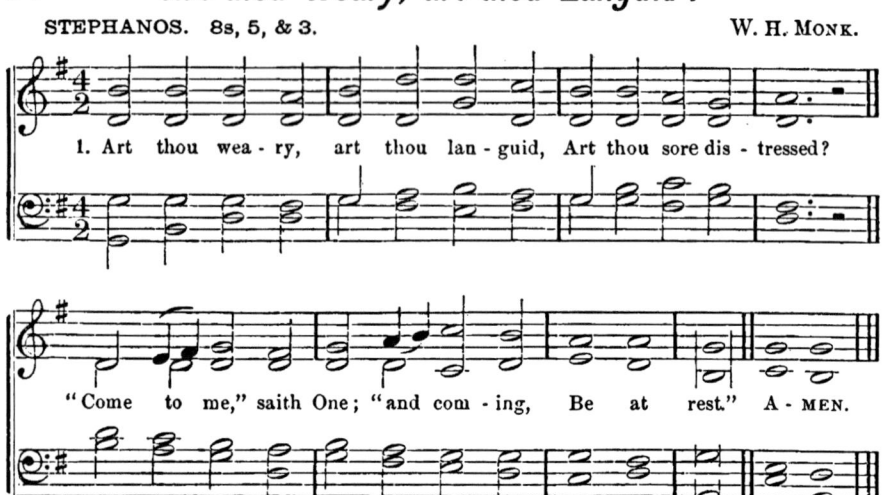

1. Art thou wea - ry, art thou lan - guid, Art thou sore dis - tressed?

"Come to me," saith One; "and com - ing, Be at rest." A - MEN.

2 Hath He marks to lead me to Him
    If He be my Guide?
  "In His feet and hands are wound-
      prints,
    And His side."

3 Is there diadem, as Monarch,
    That His brow adorns?
  "Yea, a crown in very surety,
     But of thorns."

4 If I find Him, if I follow,
    What His guerdon here?
  "Many a sorrow, many a labor,
     Many a tear."

5 If I still hold closely to Him,
    What hath He at last?
  "Sorrow vanquished, labor ended,
     Jordan passed."

6 If I ask Him to receive me,
    Will he say me nay?
  "Not till earth and not till heaven
     Pass away."

7 Finding, following, keeping, struggling,
    Is He sure to bless?
  "Saints, apostles, prophets, martyrs,
     Answer, Yes."   AMEN.

St. Stephen the Sabaite, 775.   Trans. by Neale.

55   *Jesus, my Shepherd, let me Share.*

GRACE CHURCH.   L. M.   L. PLEYEL.

1. Je-sus, my Shepherd, let me share Thy guiding hand, Thy ten-der care;

GRACE CHURCH.—Continued.

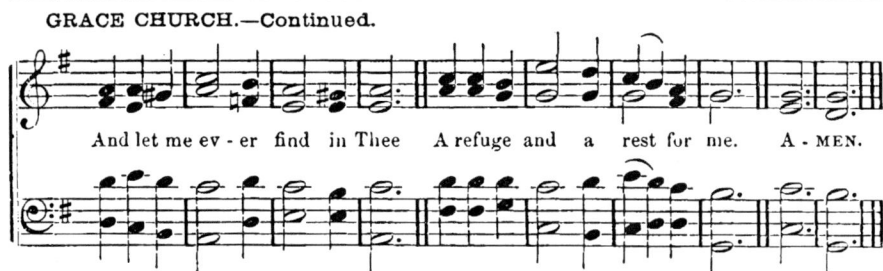

And let me ev - er find in Thee   A refuge and a rest for me.   A - MEN.

2 Oh lead me ever by Thy side
  Where fields are green and waters glide,
  And be Thou still, where'er I be,
  A refuge and a rest for me.

3 While I this barren desert tread,
  Feed Thou my soul on heavenly bread;

'Mid foes and fears Thee may I see,
  A refuge and a rest for me.

4 When death shall end this mortal strife,
  Bring me through death to endless life;
  Then, face to face beholding Thee,
  My refuge and my rest shall be. AMEN.

56   *Thou who on that Wondrous Journey.*

INVITATION.   8s & 5s.   From *Catholic Hymns.*

1. Thou who on that wondrous jour - ney Sett'st Thy face to die,

By Thy ho - ly meek ex - am - ple Teach us char - i - ty.   A - MEN.

2 Thou who that dread cup of suffering
  Didst not put from Thee,
O most loving of the loving,
  Give us charity.

3 Thou who reignest, bright in glory,
  On God's throne on high,

Oh, that we may share Thy triumph,
  Grant us charity.

4 Send us faith that trusts Thy promise,
  Hope with upward eye,
But, more blest than both, and greater,
  Send us charity. AMEN.

Henry Alford, 1866.

57   *We Sing the Praise of Him who Died.*

MELCOMBE. **L. M.**   SAMUEL WEBBE.

1. We sing the praise of Him who died, Of Him who died up-

on the cross; The sin - ner's Hope let men de - ride:

For this we count the world but loss. A - MEN.

2 Inscribed upon the cross we see
  In shining letters, "God is love;"
He bears our sins upon the tree,
  He brings us mercy from above.

3 The cross! it takes our guilt away,
  It holds the fainting spirit up,
It cheers with hope the gloomy day,
  And sweetens every bitter cup.

4 It makes the coward spirit brave,
  And nerves the feeble arm for fight,

It takes its terror from the grave,
  And gilds the bed of death with light.

5 The balm of life, the cure of woe,
  The measure and the pledge of love,
The sinner's refuge here below,
  The angels' theme in heaven above.

6 To Christ, who won for sinners grace
  By bitter grief and anguish sore,
Be praise from all the ransomed race,
  For ever and for evermore. AMEN.
                                Thomas Kelly, 1815.

58 *My Faith Looks up to Thee.*

OLIVET. 6s & 4s.   LOWELL MASON.

1. My faith looks up to Thee, Thou Lamb of Cal-va-ry, Sa-viour di-vine:

Now hear me while I pray; Take all my guilt a-way;

Oh, let me from this day Be whol-ly Thine. A-MEN.

2 May Thy rich grace impart
Strength to my fainting heart,
  My zeal inspire;
As Thou hast died for me,
Oh, may my love to Thee
Pure, warm, and changeless be,
  A living fire.

3 While life's dark maze I tread,
And griefs around me spread,
  Be Thou my Guide;

Bid darkness turn to day,
Wipe sorrow's tears away,
Nor let me ever stray
  From Thee aside.

4 When ends life's transient dream,
When death's cold, sullen stream
  Shall o'er me roll,
Blest Saviour, then, in love,
Fear and distrust remove;
Oh, bear me safe above,
  A ransomed soul.   AMEN.

Ray Palmer.

59   *Jesus, to Thy Cross I Hasten.*

OSGOOD.   8s, 7s, & 4.

1. Je - sus, to Thy cross I hast-eu, In all wear - i - ness my home ; }
Let Thy dy- ing love come o'er me— Light and cov - ert in the gloom: }

Sa - viour, hide me, Sa - viour, hide me, Till the hour of

gloom is o'er, Till the hour of gloom is o'er. A - MEN.

2 When life's tempests dark are rolling
  Fearful shadows o'er my way,
Let firm faith in Thee sustain me,
  Every rising fear allay;
    Hide, oh hide me,
Hide me till the storm is o'er.

3 When stern death at last shall lead me
  Through the dark and lonely vale,
Let Thy hope uphold and cheer me,
  Though my flesh and heart should fail;
    Safely hide me
With Thyself for evermore. AMEN.

60   *I Lay my Sins on Jesus.*

MIRIAM.   7s & 6s. D.   J. P. HOLBROOK.

1. I lay my sins on Je - , sus, The spot - less Lamb of God;

He bears them all, and frees us   From the ac - curs - ed load;
D.S. White in His blood most pre - cious, Till not a spot re - mains.

I bring my guilt to Je - sus, To wash my crim-son stains   A - MEN.

2 I lay my wants on Jesus:
   All fullness dwells in Him;
  He heals all my diseases,
   He doth my soul redeem;
  I lay my griefs on Jesus,
   My burdens and my cares:
  He from them all releases,
   He all my sorrows shares.

3 I long to be like Jesus,
   Meek, loving, lowly, mild;
  I long to be like Jesus,
   The Father's holy Child;
  I long to be with Jesus
   Amid the heavenly throng,
  To sing with saints His praises,
   To learn the angels' song.   AMEN.
                                  H. Bonar.

61 *All Glory, Laud, and Honor.*

ST. THEODULPH. 7s & 6s.   M. TESCHNER, 1613.

1. All glo - ry, laud, and hon - or To Thee, Redeem-er, King,)
To whom the lips of chil - dren Made sweet ho-san-nas ring!) A - MEN.

2. Thou art the King of Is - rael, Thou Da - vid's roy - al Son,
3. The com - pa - ny, etc.

Who in the Lord's name com - est, The King and bless - ed One.

3 The company of angels
 Are praising Thee on high,
And mortal men, and all things
 Created, make reply. All glory, etc.

4 The people of the Hebrews
 With palms before Thee went;
Our praise and prayer and anthems
 Before Thee we present. All glory, etc.

5 To Thee, before Thy passion,
 They sang their hymns of praise;
To Thee, now high-exalted,
 Our melody we raise. All glory, etc.

6 Thou didst accept their praises;
 Accept the prayers we bring,
Who in all good delightest,
 Thou good and gracious King.
   All glory, etc. AMEN.
   Trans. by Jno. M. Neale, 1856.

62 *When, His Salvation Bringing.*

MEHUL. 7s & 6s.　　　　　　　　　　　　　　From MEHUL.

1. When, His sal - va - tion bring - ing, To Si - on Je - sus came, }
   The chil - dren all stood sing - ing Ho - san - na to His name; }

D.C. He let them still at - tend Him, And smiled to hear their song.

Nor did their zeal of - fend Him, But as He rode a - long,

CHORUS for each verse.

Ho - san - na! Ho - san - na to Je - sus they sang. A MEN.

2 And since the Lord retaineth
　His love to children still,
Though now as King He reigneth
　On Sion's heavenly hill,
We'll flock around His banner
　Who sits upon the throne,
And cry aloud, "Hosanna
　To David's royal Son!"
　　Hosanna to Jesus we'll sing.

3 For should we fail proclaiming
　Our great Redeemer's praise,
The stones, our silence shaming,
　Might well hosannahs raise.
But shall we only render
　The tribute of our words?
No! while our hearts are tender,
　They too shall be the Lord's.
　　Hosanna to Jesus our King. AMEN.
　　　　　　　　　　J. King.

63   *Hosanna! Raise the Pealing Hymn.*

ST. PETER.   C. M.   A. R. REINAGLE.

1. Ho - san - na! Raise the peal - ing hymn To Da - vid's Son and Lord;

With cher- u- bim and ser - a-phim Ex - alt th' incarnate Word. A - MEN.

2 Hosanna! Sovereign, Prophet, Priest!
  How vast Thy gifts! how free!
Thy blood our life, Thy word our feast,
  Thy name our only plea.

3 Hosanna, Master! Lo, we bring
  Our off'rings to Thy throne;
Not gold, nor myrrh, nor mortal thing,
  But hearts to be Thine own.

4 Hosanna! Once Thy gracious ear
  Approved a lisping throng;
Be gracious still, and deign to hear
  Our poor but grateful song.

5 O Saviour! if, redeemed by Thee,
  Thy temple we behold,
Hosannas through eternity
  We'll sing to harps of gold. AMEN.

Wm. H. Havergal, 1833.

64   *Come, let us Join our Cheerful Songs.*

SALISBURY.   C. M.   From RAVENSCROFT'S *Psalter.*

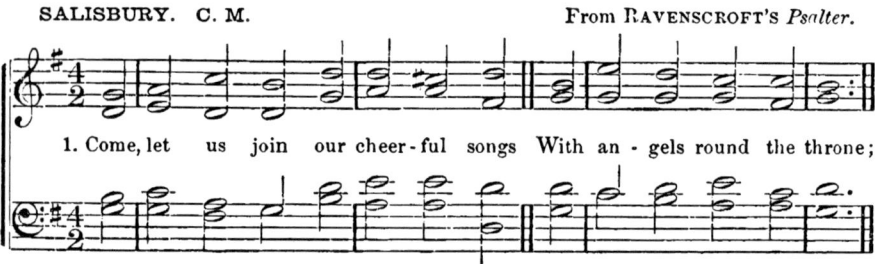

1. Come, let us join our cheer - ful songs With an - gels round the throne;

SALISBURY.—Continued.

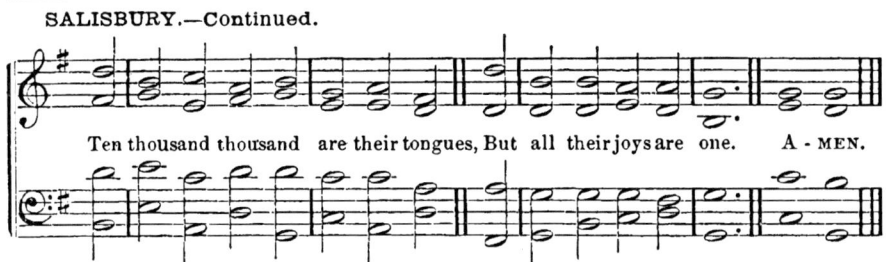

Ten thousand thousand are their tongues, But all their joys are one. A - MEN.

2 "Worthy the Lamb that died," they cry,
  "To be exalted thus!"
  "Worthy the Lamb," our lips reply,
  "For He was slain for us!"

3 Jesus is worthy to receive
  Honor and power divine,

And blessings more than we can give
  Be, Lord, for ever Thine.

4 Let all creation join in one
  To bless the sacred name
Of Him that sits upon the throne,
  And to adore the Lamb. AMEN.

Isaac Watts.

65   *Ride on! Ride on in Majesty!*

ROUSSEAU. L. M.   W. W. ROUSSEAU.

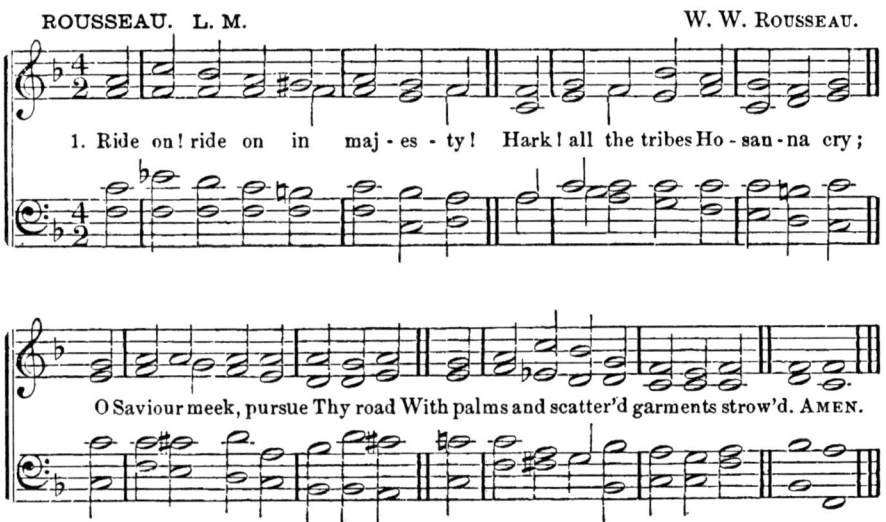

1. Ride on! ride on in maj-es-ty! Hark! all the tribes Ho-san-na cry;

O Saviour meek, pursue Thy road With palms and scatter'd garments strow'd. AMEN.

2 Ride on! ride on in majesty!
In lowly pomp ride on to die;
O Christ, Thy triumphs now begin
O'er captive death and conquered sin.

3 Ride on! ride on in majesty!
In lowly pomp ride on to die;
Bow Thy meek head to mortal pain,
Then take, O God, Thy power and reign.
AMEN.

Henry H. Milman, 1827.

66   *Behold the Sin-Atoning Lamb.*

FEDERAL STREET. L. M.   H. K. OLIVER.

1. Be-hold the sin - a - ton-ing Lamb With wonder, grat - i-tude and love; To take a - way our guilt and shame See Him de - scend - ing from a - bove. A - MEN.

2 Our sins and griefs on Him were laid:
  He meekly bore the mighty load;
Our ransom-price He fully paid
  In groans and tears, in sweat and blood.

3 To save a guilty world He dies;
  Sinners, behold the bleeding Lamb!
To Him lift up your longing eyes,
  And hope for mercy in His name.

4 Pardon and peace through Him abound,
  He can the richest blessings give;
Salvation in His name is found,
  He bids the dying sinner live.

5 Jesus, my Lord, I look to Thee:
  Where else can helpless sinners go?
Thy boundless love shall set me free
  From all my wretchedness and woe.
                  AMEN.

67   *Now, my Soul, Thy Voice Upraising.*

SANTOLIUS.   8s & 7s. D.   German.

1. Now, my soul, thy voice up - rais - ing, Tell in sweet and mournful strain)
How the Cru - ci - fied, en - dur - ing Grief and wounds and dy - ing pain, ∫

Free - ly of His love was of - fered, Sin - less was for sin-ners slain,

Free-ly of His love was of - fered, Sinless was for sin-ners slain.   A - MEN.

2 See! His hands and feet are fastened :
   So He makes His people free ;
Not a wound whence blood is flowing
   But a fount of grace shall be ;
‖: Yea, the very nails which nail Him
   Nail us also to the tree. :‖

3 Through His heart the spear is piercing;
   Though His foes have seen Him die,
Blood and water thence are streaming
   In a tide of mystery—

‖: Water from our guilt to cleanse us,
   Blood to win us crowns on high. :‖

4 Jesus, may those precious fountains
   Drink to thirsting souls afford ;
Let them be our cup and healing,
   And at length our full reward ;
‖: So a ransomed world shall ever
   Praise Thee, its redeeming Lord. :‖
                   AMEN.

Santolius Maglorianus, 1650.   Trans. by Hy. Wm. Baker, 1861.

68   *O Sacred Head now Wounded.*

BACH. 7s & 6s.   " O Haupt voll Blutt und Wunden."   Arr. by H. S.

1. O Sa - cred Head now wound - ed, With grief and shame weigh'd down;
Now scorn - ful - ly sur - round - ed, With thorns Thy on - ly crown;

O Sa - cred Head, what glo - ry, What bliss, till now, was Thine!

Yet, tho' despised and go - ry, I joy to call Thee mine. A-MEN.

2 O noblest brow and dearest—
  In other days the world
All feared when Thou appearedst—
  What shame on Thee is hurled!
How art Thou pale with anguish,
  With sore abuse and scorn!
How does that visage languish
  Which once was bright as morn!

3 What Thou, my Lord, hast suffered
  Was all for sinners' gain;
Mine, mine was the transgression,
  But Thine the deadly pain.

Lo! here I fall, my Saviour:
  'Tis I deserve Thy place;
Look on me with Thy favor,
  Vouchsafe to me Thy grace

4 The joy can ne'er be spoken,
  Above all joys beside,
When, in Thy body broken,
  I thus with safety hide.
Lord of my life, desiring
  Thy glory now to see,
Beside Thy cross expiring,
  I'd breathe my soul to Thee.

5 What language shall I borrow
  To thank Thee, dearest Friend,
For this Thy dying sorrow,
  Thy pity without end?
Oh make me Thine for ever;
  And should I fainting be,
Lord, let me never, never
  Outlive my love for Thee.

6 Be near me when I'm dying,
  Oh show Thy cross to me;
And to my succor flying,
  Come, Lord, and set me free.
These eyes, new faith receiving,
  From Jesus shall not move,
For he who dies believing
  Dies safely through Thy love. AMEN.

Paul Gerhart, 1656.

69 *Glory be to Jesus.*

CASNELL. 6s & 5s.   W. H. MONK.

1. Glo - ry be to Je - sus, Who, in bit - ter pains,

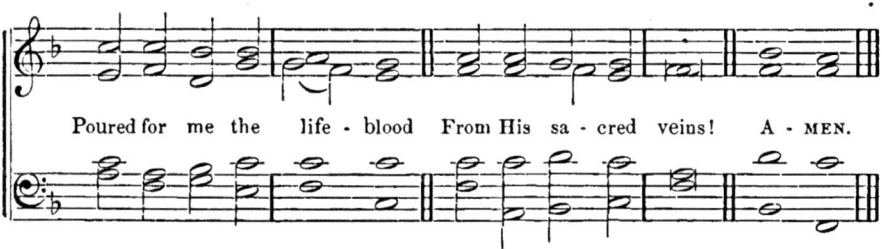

Poured for me the life - blood From His sa - cred veins! A - MEN.

2 Grace and life eternal
  In that blood I find;
Blest be His compassion,
  Infinitely kind.

3 Blest through endless ages
  Be the precious stream
Which from endless torments
  Did the world redeem.

4 Abel's blood for vengeance
  Pleaded to the skies,
But the blood of Jesus
  For our pardon cries.

5 Oft as it is sprinkled
  On our guilty hearts,
Satan in confusion,
  Terror-struck, departs.

6 Oft as earth, exulting,
  Wafts its praise on high,
Angel-hosts, rejoicing,
  Make their glad reply.

7 Lift ye, then, your voices,
  Swell the mighty flood,
And with saints and angel
  Praise the precious blood. AMEN.

Italian Hymn. Trans. E. Caswall, 1849.

6

70   *When I Survey the Wondrous Cross.*

ROCKINGHAM. L. M.   Dr. MILLER.

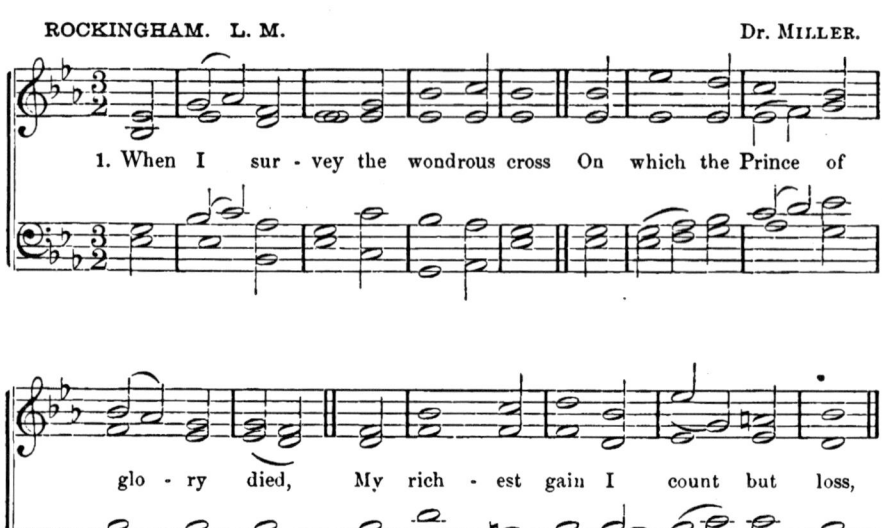

1. When I sur - vey the wondrous cross On which the Prince of

glo - ry died, My rich - est gain I count but loss,

And pour con - tempt on - all my pride. , A - MEN.

2 Forbid it, Lord, that I should boast,
   Save in the cross of Christ my God;
All the vain things that charm me
      most,
   I sacrifice them to Thy blood.

3 See, from His head, His hands, His
      feet,
   Sorrow and love flow mingled down;

Did e'er such love and sorrow meet,
   Or thorns compose a Saviour's crown?

4 Were the whole realm of Nature mine
   That were a tribute far too small;
Love so amazing, so divine,
   Demands my life, my soul, my all.
                              AMEN.
                         Isaac Watts.

71   *For ever Here my Best shall be.*

ST. AGNES.   C. M.   Dr. DYKES.

1. For ev - er here my rest shall be, Close to Thy

wound - ed side; This all my hope and all my plea —

For me the Sa - viour died. A - MEN.

2 My dying Saviour and my God,
   Fountain for guilt and sin,
Sprinkle me ever with Thy blood,
   And cleanse and keep me clean.

3 Wash me, and make me thus Thine
   own ;
   Wash me, and mine Thou art ;

Wash me, but not my feet alone,
   My hands, my head, my heart.

4 Th' atonement of Thy blood apply
   Till faith to sight improve,
Till hope in full fruition die,
   And all my soul be love. AMEN.

Charles Wesley, 1740.

72   *The Lord of Life is Risen.*

RESURRECTION.   7s & 6s. D.   A. NEVIN.

1. The Lord of life is ris - en; Sing, East - er her - alds, sing!

He bursts His rock - y pris - on; Wide let the tri - umph ring.

In death no long - er ly - ing, He rose, the Prince, to - day;

Life of the dead and dy - ing, He triumphed o'er de - cay.   A - MEN.

2 The Lord of life is risen,
  And love no longer grieves;
In ruin lies death's prison;
  Sing, heralds! Jesus lives.
We hear Thy blessed greeting,
  Salvation's work is done;
We worship Thee, repeating,
  "Life for the dead is won."

3 Around Thy tomb, O Jesus,
  How sweet the Easter breath!
Hear we not in the breezes,
  "Where is thy sting, O Death?"
Dark hell flies in commotion,
  The heavens their anthems sing,
While far o'er earth and ocean
  Glad hallelujahs ring.

4 Oh publish this salvation,
  Ye heralds, through the earth;
To every buried nation
  Proclaim the day of birth,
Till, rising from their slumbers
  In long and ancient night,
The countless heathen numbers
  Shall hail the Easter light.

5 Hail! hail! our Jesus risen!
  Sing, ransomed brethren, sing!
Through death's dark, gloomy prison
  Let Easter chorals ring.
Haste, haste, ye captive legions,
  Accept your glad reprieve;
Come forth from sin's dark regions,
  In Jesus' kingdom live. AMEN.

F. J. P. Lange, 1851. Trans. by H. Harbaugh.

73 *The Lord is Risen Indeed.*

OLNEY. S. M. Dr. L. MASON.

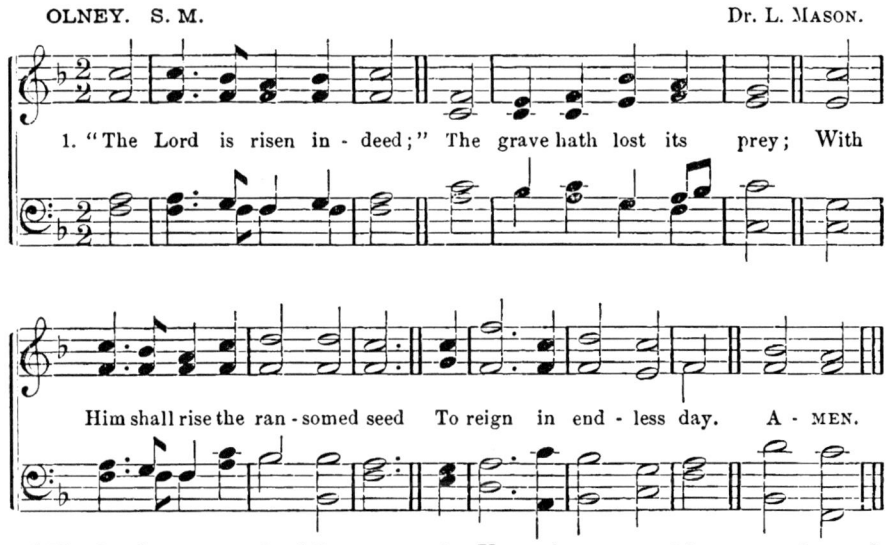

1. "The Lord is risen in - deed;" The grave hath lost its prey; With

Him shall rise the ran - somed seed To reign in end - less day. A - MEN.

2 "The Lord is risen indeed;"
  He lives, to die no more;
He lives His people's cause to plead,
  Whose curse and shame He bore.

3 "The Lord is risen indeed;"
  Attending angels, hear;

Up to the courts of heaven with speed
  The joyful tidings bear.

4 Then take your golden lyres,
  And strike each cheerful chord;
Join all the bright, celestial choirs
  To sing our risen Lord. AMEN.

Kelly.

74　　　Yes, the Redeemer Rose.

HARWICH. H. M.

1. Yes, the Re-deem-er rose, The Sa-viour left the dead, And o'er our hellish foes High raised His conquering head: In wild dis-may the guards a-round Fall to the ground and sink a-way. A - MEN.

2 Lo! the angelic bands
  In full assembly meet,
To wait His high commands
  And worship at His feet;
Joyful they come, and wing their way
From realms of day to Jesus' tomb.

3 Then back to heaven they fly,
  And the glad tidings bear;
Hark! as they soar on high
  What music fills the air!
Their anthems say, "Jesus, who bled,
Hath left the dead; He rose to-day."

4 Ye mortals, catch the sound,
  Redeemed by Him from hell,

And send the echo round
  The globe on which you dwell;
Transported, cry, "Jesus, who bled,
Hath left the dead, no more to die."

5 All hail, triumphant Lord,
  Who sav'st us with Thy blood;
Wide be Thy name adored,
  Thou rising, reigning God;
With · Thee we rise, with Thee we
  reign,
And empires gain beyond the skies.
　　　　　　　　　　　AMEN.

Philip Doddridge, 1740.

75 *The Day of Resurrection.*

SALVATORI. 7s & 6s. ·HAYDN.

1. The day of res - ur - rec - tion! Earth, tell it out a - broad!
The Pass - ov - er of glad - ness, The Pass - ov - er of God!

D.C. Our Christ hath brought us o - ver, With hymns of vic - to - ry.

From death to life e - ter - nal, From earth un-to the sky, A - MEN.

2 Our hearts, be pure from evil
  That we may see aright
The Lord in rays eternal
  Of resurrection light,
And listening to His accents
  May hear, so calm and plain,
His own "All hail!" and, hearing,
  May raise the victor strain.

3 Now let the heavens be joyful,
  Let earth her song begin,
Let all the world keep triumph,
  And all that is therein;
In grateful exultation
  Their notes let all things blend,
For Christ the Lord hath risen,
  Our Joy that hath no end. AMEN.

St. John Damascene. Trans. Dr. Doddridge, 1780.

76 *Alleluia! Alleluia!*

Rev. GERARD COBB.

1. Al - le - lu - ia! Al - le - lu - ia! Float-ing o'er the crys - tal sea,

ALLELUIA! ALLELUIA!—Continued.

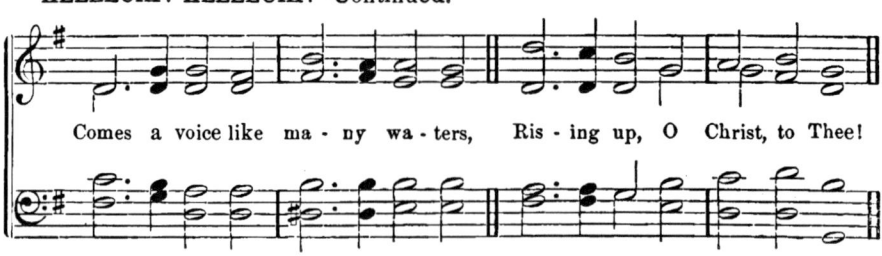

Comes a voice like ma-ny wa-ters, Ris-ing up, O Christ, to Thee!

Al-le-lu-ia! Lord al-might-y! Thou hast bought us with Thy blood;

By Thy ran-som-price of pas-sion, We approach Thee, Christ our God. A-MEN.

2 Alleluia! Alleluia!
　　From the sons of Adam rise
　Sounds of resurrection triumph,
　　Upward to the Easter skies;
　Alleluia, well beloved,
　　We receive Thee, Jesu Christ;
　Earth's ten thousand voices thunder
　　One united Eucharist.

3 Alleluia! Alleluia!
　　Welcome, Child of Mary's womb;
　Thou hast triumphed, God incarnate,
　　O'er the dungeon of the tomb;

　Alleluia! hell's battalions
　　In the light of Easter morn
　Know their brazen portals broken
　　By our Prince, the Virgin-born.

4 Alleluia! Alleluia!
　　Lamb of God, enthronèd Priest;
　Christ our Passover is offered,
　　Therefore let us keep the feast;
　Alleluia! Christ is risen!
　　Earth and heaven together sing;
　Alleluia! Alleluia!
　　Alleluia! Christ our King. AMEN.

77   *Christ the Lord is Risen to-day.*

Dr. Ions.

1. Christ the Lord is risen to - day, Sons of men and an - gels say;

Raise your joys and triumphs high, Sing, ye heavens, and, earth, re - ply.

Hal - le - lu - jah, hal - le - lu - jah, hal - le - lu - jah.   A - MEN.

2 Love's redeeming work is done,
  Fought the fight, the battle won;
  Lo! our Sun's eclipse is o'er,
  Lo! He sets in blood no more.
  Hallelujah, etc.

3 Vain the stone, the watch, the seal,
  Christ hath burst the gates of hell;
  Death in vain forbids His rise,
  Christ hath opened Paradise.
  Hallelujah, etc.

4 Lives again our glorious King;
  Where, O Death, is now thy sting?
  Once He died our souls to save;
  Where thy victory, O grave?
  Hallelujah, etc.

5 Soar we now where Christ has led,
  Following our exalted Head;
  Made like Him, like Him we rise,
  Ours the cross, the grave, the skies.
  Hallelujah, etc. AMEN.

78   *Come, ye Faithful.*

ARTHUR SULLIVAN.

1. Come, ye faithful, raise the strain   Of tri-umph-ant glad-ness;

God hath brought His Is-ra-el   In-to joy from sad-ness:

Loosed from Pharaoh's bit-ter yoke   Ja-cob's sons and daugh-ters;

Led them with unmoistened foot Through the Red Sea wa-ters.   A-MEN.

2 'Tis the spring of souls to-day ;
   Christ hath burst His prison,
And from three days' sleep in death
   As a Sun hath risen ;
All the winter of our sins,
   Long and dark, is flying
From His light to whom we give
   Laud and praise undying.

3 Now the queen of seasons, bright
   With the day of splendor,
With the royal feast of feasts,
   Comes its joy to render—

Comes to glad Jerusalem,
   Who with true affection
Welcomes in unwearied strains
   Jesus' resurrection.

4 Alleluia ! now we cry
   To our King immortal,
Who triumphant burst the bars
   Of the tomb's dark portal :
Alleluia with the Son
   God the Father praising ;
Alleluia yet again
   To the Spirit raising.   AMEN.

79   *Jesus Christ is Risen to-day.*

WORGAN. 7s.   CAREY, 1743.

1. Je - sus Christ is risen to - day, Al - - - - - le-
lu - ia ! Our tri - umph - ant, ho - ly day,
Al - - - - le - - lu - ia ! Who did once up - on the cross,

WORGAN.—Continued.

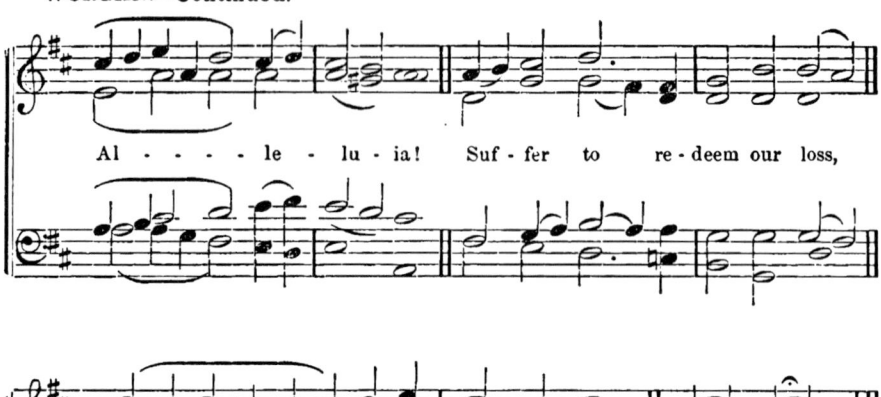

Al - - - le - lu - ia! Suf - fer to re - deem our loss,

Al - - - - - le - - lu - ia! A - MEN.

2 Hymns of praise, then, let us sing
Unto Christ, our heavenly King,
Who endured the cross and grave
Sinners to redeem and save.
> Alleluia!

3 But the pains which He endured
Our salvation have procured;
Now above the sky He's King,
Where the angels ever sing
> Alleluia! AMEN.

80   *The World itself keeps Easter Day.*

Music by GEO. WM. WARREN.

Unison or Parts.
mf Animato.

1. The world it- self keeps Easter day, And Easter larks are singing, And Easter flow'rs are

THE WORLD ITSELF KEEPS EASTER DAY.—Continued.

blooming gay, And Easter buds are springing.　　Hal - le - lu - jah, Hal - le - lu - jah!

Organ.

The Lord of all things lives a - new, And all His works are

ris - ing too. Hal - le - lu - jah, Hal - le - lu - jah, Hal - le - lu - jah!

2 There stood three Marys by the tomb
　On Easter morning early,
When day had scarcely chased the
　　gloom,
　And dew was white and pearly.
　　Hallelujah! hallelujah!
With loving but with erring mind
They came the Prince of life to find.
　　Hallelujah! hallelujah!

3 But earlier still the angel sped,
　His news of comfort giving,　[dead
And "Why," he said, "among the
　Thus seek ye for the living?"
　　Hallelujah! hallelujah!

"Go tell them all, and make them
　　blest;
Tell Peter first, and then the rest."
　　Hallelujah! hallelujah!

4 The world itself keeps Easter day,
　And Easter larks are singing,
And Easter flowers are blooming gay,
　And Easter buds are springing;
　　Hallelujah! hallelujah!
*The Lord hath risen, as all things tell;
Good Christians, see ye rise as well.
　　Hallelujah! hallelujah!

* Sing these last two lines slower, with a pause at
the end of each.

81 *Welcome, Happy Morning.*

ARTHUR SULLIVAN.

1. "Wel-come, hap-py morning!" age to age shall say; Hell to - day is

vanquish'd; Heaven is won to - day; Lo! the Dead is liv - ing,

God for ev - er - more; Him, their true Cre - a - tor, all His works a - dore.

"Wel-come, hap - py morning!" age to age shall say. A - MEN.

2 Months in due succession, days of
  lengthening light,
Hours and passing moments, praise
  Thee in their flight;
Brightness of the morning, sky and
  fields and sea,
Vanquisher of darkness, bring their
  praise to Thee.
"Welcome, happy morning!" age to
  age shall say.

3 Thou, of life the Author, death didst
  undergo,
Tread the path of darkness, saving
  strength to show;
Come, then, true and faithful, now
  fulfil Thy word;
'Tis Thine own third morning; rise,
  O buried Lord!
"Welcome, happy morning!" age to
  age shall say. Amen.

82   *The Happy Morn is Come.*

ANON.

1. The hap-py morn is come; Triumphant o'er the grave, The Saviour leaves the tomb, Om-nip-o-tent to save. Cap-tiv-i-ty is cap-tive led, For Je-sus liv-eth, that was dead, For Je-sus liv-eth, that was dead.

2 Christ hath the ransom paid,
  The glorious work is done;
On Him our help is laid,
  By Him our victory won.
Captivity is captive led,
For Jesus liveth, that was dead.

3 Hail, the triumphant Lord,
  The resurrection Thou!
Hail, the incarnate Word!
  Before Thy throne we bow.
Captivity is captive led,
For Jesus liveth, that was dead.

83   *The Strife is G'er, the Battle Done.*

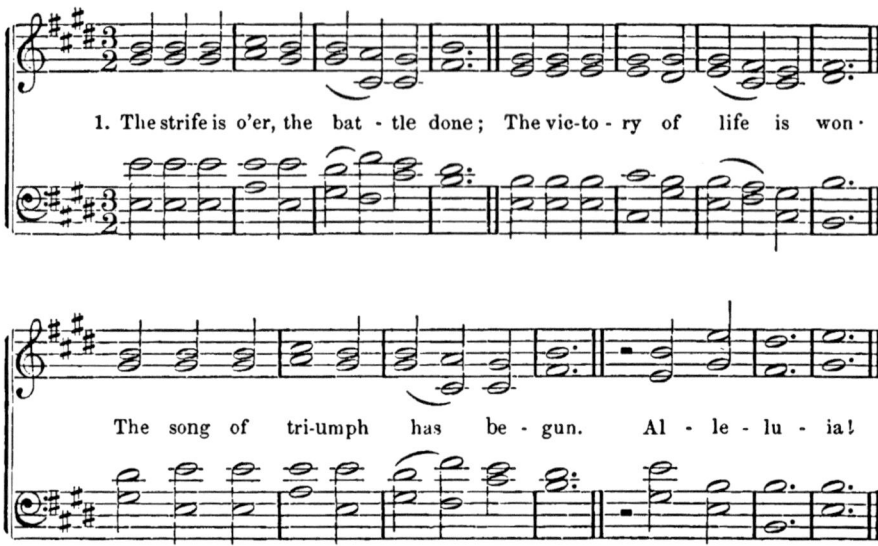

1. The strife is o'er, the bat - tle done; The vic-to - ry of life is won·

The song of tri-umph has be - gun. Al - le - lu - ia!

CHORUS to last verse.

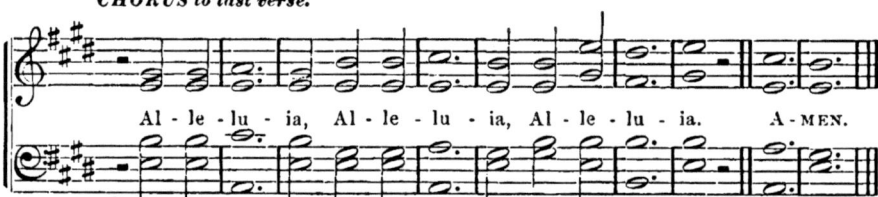

Al - le - lu - ia, Al - le - lu - ia, Al - le - lu - ia.   A - MEN.

Organ.

2 The powers of death have done their
    worst,
  But Christ their legions hath dis-
    persed;
  Let shout of holy joy outburst.
                Alleluia!

3 The three sad days are quickly sped,
  He rises glorious from the dead;
  All glory to our risen Head!
                Alleluia!

4 He closed the yawning gates of hell,
  The bars from heaven's high portals
    fe l;
  Let hymns of praise His triumphs tell.
                Alleluia!

5 Lord, by the stripes which wounded
    Thee,
  From Death's dread sting Thy servants
    free,
  That we may live and sing to Thee
             Alleluia! AMEN.

84   *Our Lord hath Arisen.*

1. Our Lord hath a - ris - en; The tempt-er is foiled, His le - gions are

scat - tered, His strongholds are spoiled. Oh sing Hal-le - lu - jah! Oh

sing Hal-le - lu - jah! Oh sing Hal-le - lu - jah! Christ Jesus is King.

2 O Death, we defy thee ;
  A stronger than thou
Hath entered thy palace ;
We fear thee not now.
      Oh sing, etc.

3 O Sin, thou art vanquished,
  Thy long reign is o'er ;

Though still thou dost vex us,
  We dread thee no more.
      Oh sing, etc.

4 Our Lord hath arisen,
  Day breaketh at last ;
The long night of weeping
Is now wellnigh past.
      Oh sing, etc.

7

85   *Crown Him with many Crowns.*

DIADEMATA.   S. M. D.   Dr. G. J. Elvey.

1. Crown Him with man - y crowns, The Lamb up - on His throne;

Hark how the heaven-ly an - them drowns All mu - sic but its own!

With His most pre - cious blood From sin He set us free

We hail Him as our matchless King Through all eter - ni - ty. A - MEN.

2 Crown Him, the Virgin's Son,
  The God incarnate born,
Whose arm those crimson trophies won
  Which now His brow adorn ;
  Fruit of the mystic rose,
The Root whence mercy ever flows,
  The Babe of Bethlehem.

3 Crown Him the Lord of love,
  Behold His hands and side,
Rich wounds, yet visible above
  In beauty glorified ;

  No angel in the sky
  Can fully bear that sight,
But downward bends his burning eye
  At mysteries so bright.

4 Crown Him the Lord of heaven,
  One with the Father known,
One with the Spirit through Him given
  From yonder glorious throne.
  To Thee be endless praise,
  For Thou for us hast died ;
Be Thou, O Lord, through endless days
  Adored and magnified. AMEN.

Matthew Bridges.

86   *The Golden Gates are Lifted up.*

HERMANN.   C. M.   N. HERMANN.

1. The gold-en gates are lift-ed up, The doors are o-pened wide,

The King of glo-ry is gone in Un-to His Father's side. A-MEN.

2 Thou art gone up before us, Lord,
  To make for us a place,
That we may be where now Thou art,
  And look upon God's face.

3 And ever on Thine earthly path
  A gleam of glory lies,
A light still breaks behind the cloud
  That veiled Thee from our eyes.

4 Lift up our hearts, lift up our minds,
  Let Thy dear grace be given,
That while we tarry here below
  Our treasure be in heaven ;

5 That where Thou art, at God's right
    hand,
  Our hope, our love, may be ;
Dwell Thou in us that we may dwell
  For evermore in Thee. AMEN.

C. F. Alexander. Altered.

87   *Hail the Day that Sees Him Rise.*

HENDON. 7s.   C. MALAN.

1. Hail the day that sees Him rise, Rav-ished from our wish-ful eyes; Christ, a while to mor-tals given, Re-as-cends His na-tive heaven, Re-as-cends His na-tive heaven. A - MEN.

2 There the pompous triumph waits;
Lift your heads, eternal gates!
Wide unfold the radiant scene,
Take the King of glory in.

3 Him though highest heaven receives,
Still He loves the earth He leaves;
Though returning to His throne,
Still He calls mankind His own.

4 See, He lifts His hands above;
See, He shows the prints of love;

Hark! His gracious lips bestow
Blessings on His Church below.

5 Still for us His death He pleads;
Prevalent, He intercedes;
Near Himself prepares our place,
Harbinger of human race.

6 There we shall with Thee remain,
Partners of Thine endless reign;
There Thy face unclouded see,
Find our heav'n of heav'ns in Thee.
                     AMEN.
Charles Wesley, 1739.

88   *Our Lord is Risen from the Dead.*

KELKER. L. M.   FRED. LUCCHESI.

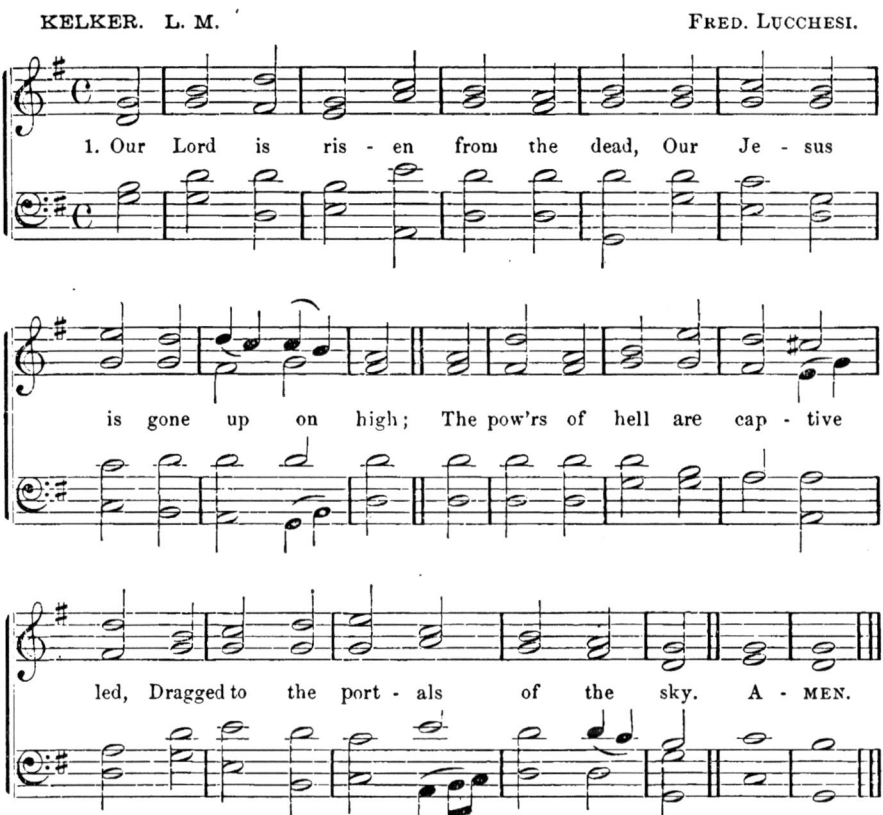

1. Our Lord is ris - en from the dead, Our Je - sus is gone up on high; The pow'rs of hell are cap - tive led, Dragged to the port - als of the sky. A - MEN.

2 There His triumphal chariot waits,
   And angels chant the solemn lay;
  Lift up your heads, ye heavenly gates;
   Ye everlasting doors, give way.

3 Loose all your bars of massy light,
   And wide unfold the radiant scene;
  He claims those mansions as His right:
   Receive the King of glory in.

4 Who is the King of glory, who?
   The Lord that all His foes o'ercame,
The world, sin, death, and hell o'erthrew,
   And Jesus is the Conqueror's name.

5 Lo! His triumphal chariot waits,
   And angels chant the solemn lay;
  Lift up your heads, ye heavenly gates;
   Ye everlasting doors, give way.

6 Who is the King of glory, who?
   The Lord, of boundless power pos-
     sessed,
  The King of saints, and angels too,
   God over all, for ever blessed. AMEN.
                         Rev. C. Wesley.

89   *Christ, above all Glory Seated.*

ASCENSION.   8s & 7s.   German.

1. Christ, a - bove all glo - ry seat - ed, King tri-

umph - ant, strong to save, Dy - ing, Thou hast death de-

feat - ed, Bur - ied, Thou hast spoiled the grave. A - MEN.

2 Thou art gone where now is given
   What no mortal sight could gain,
On th' eternal throne of heaven
   In Thy Father's power to reign.

3 There Thy kingdoms all adore Thee,
   Heaven above and earth below,
While the depths of hell before Thee,
   Trembling and amazèd, bow.

4 We, O Lord, with hearts adoring,
   Follow Thee beyond the sky;

Hear our prayers Thy grace imploring,
   Lift our souls to Thee on high.

5 So, when Thou again in glory
   On the clouds of heaven shalt shine,
We Thy flock may stand before Thee,
   Owned for evermore as Thine.

6 Hail, all hail! in Thee confiding,
   Jesus, Thee shall all adore,
In Thy Father's might abiding,
   With one Spirit evermore.   AMEN.
       Latin Hymn, Fifth Century.   Trans. (?).

90   *Come, Holy Spirit, Heavenly Dove.*

BARBY.   C. M.   W. TANSUR.

1. Come, Ho - ly Spir - it, heaven - ly Dove, With
all Thy quick - 'ning powers; Kin - dle a flame of

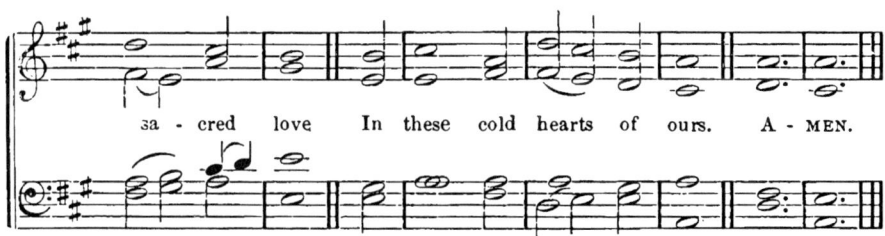

sa - cred love In these cold hearts of ours. A - MEN.

2 Look how we grovel here below,
   Fond of these trifling toys;
Our souls can neither fly nor go
   To reach eternal joys.

3 In vain we tune our formal songs,
   In vain we strive to rise;
Hosannas languish on our tongues,
   And our devotion dies.

4 Dear Lord, and shall we ever live
   At this poor dying rate?—
Our love so faint, so cold to Thee,
   And Thine to us so great?

5 Come, Holy Spirit, heavenly Dove,
   With all Thy quickening powers:
Come shed abroad a Saviour's love,
   And that shall kindle ours. AMEN.

Isaac Watts, 1709.

91 *Our Blest Redeemer, ere He Breathed.*

ST. CUTHBERT. 8s, 6, & 4.   Rev. Dr. DYKES.

1. Our blest Re-deem - er, ere He breathed His ten - der last fare- well,

A Guide, a Com-fort - er, bequeathed With us to dwell. A - MEN.

2 He came in semblance of a dove
  With sheltering wings outspread,
The holy balm of peace and love
  On earth to shed.

3 He came sweet influence to impart,
  A gracious, willing Guest
While He can find one humble heart
  Wherein to rest.

4 And His that gentle voice we hear,
  Soft as the breath of even,

That checks each thought, that calms
  each fear,
  And speaks of heaven.

5 And every virtue we possess,
  And every victory won,
And every thought of holiness,
  Are His alone.

6 Spirit of purity and grace,
  Our weakness, pitying, see;
Oh make our hearts Thy dwelling-place,
  And meet for Thee. AMEN.
             Harriet Auber.

92 *Come, Gracious Spirit, Heavenly Dove.*

WARD. L. M.   Arr. by LOWELL MASON.

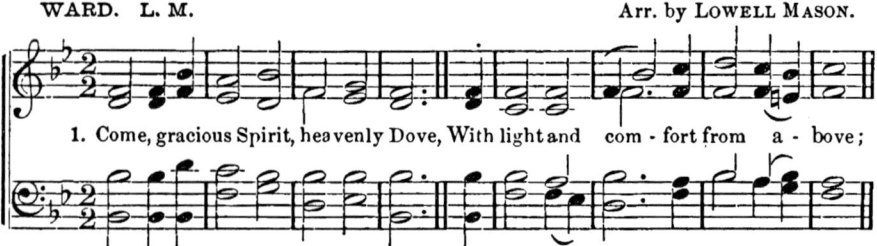

1. Come, gracious Spirit, heavenly Dove, With light and com - fort from a - bove;

WARD.—Continued.

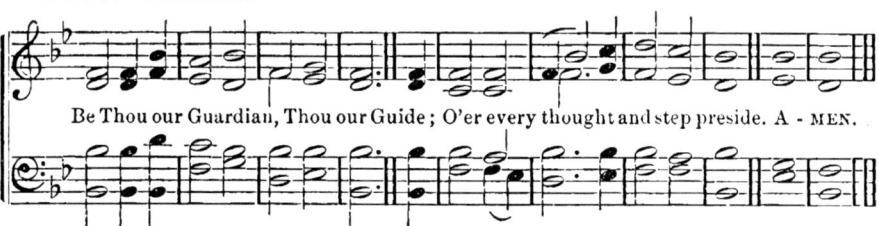

Be Thou our Guardian, Thou our Guide; O'er every thought and step preside. A - MEN.

2 Conduct us safe, conduct us far,
  From every sin and hurtful snare;
  Lead to Thy word, that rules must give
  And teach us lessons how to live.

3 The light of truth to us display,
  And make us know and choose Thy way;
  Plant holy fear in every heart,
  That we from God may ne'er depart.

4 Lead us to Christ, the living Way,
  Nor let us from His precepts stray;
  Lead us to holiness, the road
  That we must take to dwell with God.

5 Lead us to heaven, that we may share
  Fullness of joy for ever there;
  Lead us to God, our final rest,
  To be with Him for ever blest. AMEN.

Simon Browne, 1720. Altered.

93   *Gracious Spirit! Love Divine!*

ST. MARTIN.   7s.   Old French Melody.

1. Gra- cious Spir-it! Love di - vine! Let Thy light with-in me shine; All my

guilt - y fears re - move, Fill me full of heaven and love. A - MEN.

2 Speak Thy pardoning grace to me,
  Set the burdened sinner free;
  Lead me to the Lamb of God,
  Wash me in His precious blood.

3 Life and peace to me impart,
  Seal salvation on my heart;

  Breathe Thyself into my breast,
  Earnest of immortal rest.

4 Let me never from Thee stray,
  Keep me in the narrow way;
  Fill my soul with joy divine,
  Keep me, Lord, for ever Thine. AMEN.

John Stocker, 1776.

94   *Come, Holy Spirit, Come.*

STATE STREET. S. M.   I. C. WOODMAN.

1. Come, Ho - ly Spir - it, come, Let Thy bright beams a - rise; Dis - pel the darkness from our minds, And o - pen all our eyes. A - MEN.

2 Revive our drooping faith,
  Our doubts and fears remove,
And kindle in our breasts the flame
  Of never-dying love.

3 Convince us of our sin,
  Then lead to Jesus' blood,
And to our wondering view reveal
  The secret love of God.

4 'Tis Thine to cleanse the heart,
  To sanctify the soul,
To pour fresh life in every part,
  And new-create the whole.

5 Dwell, therefore, in our hearts,
  Our minds from bondage free;
Then we shall know and praise and
    love
The Father, Son, and Thee. AMEN.

Joseph Hart, 1759.

95   *The Spirit in our Hearts.*

OLMUTZ. S. M.   Arr. by LOWELL MASON.

1. The Spir - it in our hearts Is whispering, "Sin - ner, come!"

OLMUTZ.—Continued.

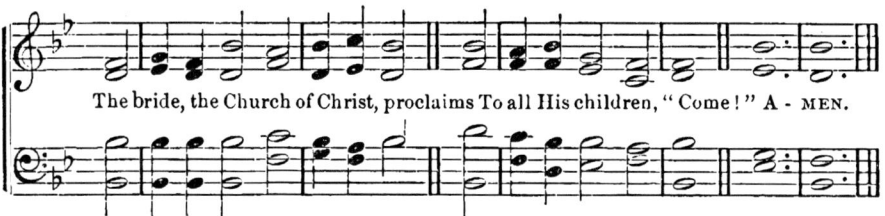

The bride, the Church of Christ, proclaims To all His children, "Come!" A - MEN.

2 Let him that heareth say
    To all about him, "Come!"
Let him that thirsts for righteousness
    To Christ, the Fountain, come.

3 Yes, whosoever will,
    Oh, let him freely come,

And freely drink the stream of life;
    'Tis Jesus bids him come.

4 Lo! Jesus, who invites,
    Declares, "I quickly come;"
Lord, even so; I wait Thine hour;
    Jesus, my Saviour, come. AMEN.

Bp. H. N. Onderdonk, 1826.

96   *Holy Ghost, the Infinite.*

PARACLETE. 7s & 5.

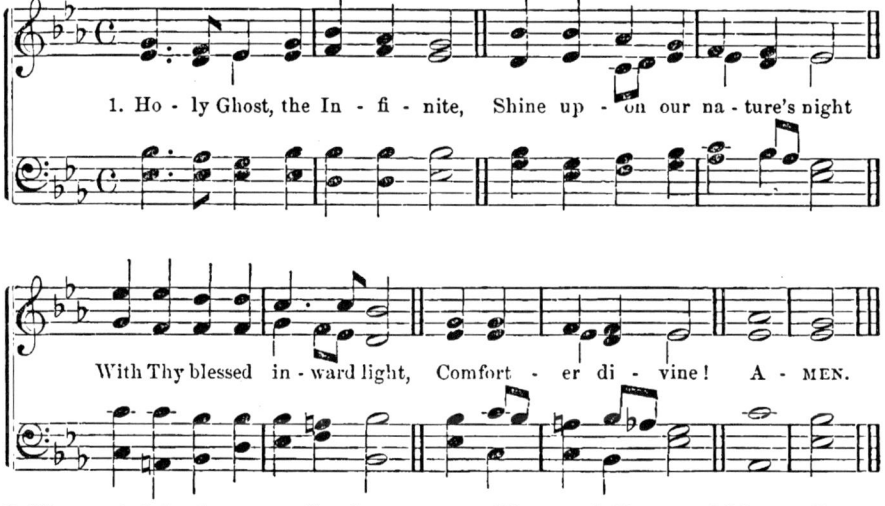

1. Ho - ly Ghost, the In - fi - nite,   Shine up - on our na - ture's night

With Thy blessed in - ward light,   Comfort - er di - vine!   A - MEN.

2 We are sinful: cleanse us, Lord;
    We are faint: Thy strength afford;
Lost, until by Thee restored,
    Comforter divine!

3 Like the dew Thy peace distill,
    Guide, subdue our wayward will,

Things of Christ unfolding still,
    Comforter divine!

4 Search for us the depths of God,
    Bear us up the starry road
To the height of Thine abode,
    Comforter divine! AMEN.

97   *Holy, Holy, Holy, Lord God Almighty!*

NICÆA.   11, 12s, & 10.   Rev. Dr. DYKES.

1. Ho - ly, Ho - ly, Ho - ly, Lord God al - might - y!

Ear - ly in the morn - ing our song shall rise to Thee:

Ho - ly, Ho - ly, Ho - ly, Mer - ci - ful and Might - y!

God in three Per - sons, bless - ed Trin - i - ty!   A - MEN.

2 Holy, Holy, Holy! All the saints adore Thee,
  Casting down their golden crowns around the glassy sea,
  Cherubim and seraphim falling down before Thee,
  Which wert, and art, and evermore shalt be.

* The small notes are intended for the second and third verses.

3 Holy, Holy, Holy! though the darkness hide Thee,
  Though the eye of sinful man Thy glory may not see,
  Only Thou art holy; there is none beside Thee
  Perfect in power, in love, and purity.

4 Holy, Holy, Holy! Lord God almighty!
  All Thy works shall praise Thy name, in earth and sky and sea;
  Holy, Holy, Holy! Merciful and Mighty,
  God in three Persons, blessed Trinity! AMEN.

Bishop Heber.

98 *Holy, Holy, Holy Lord.*

HALLETT. 7s. 6 lines.   J. H. SHEPHERD.

1. Ho-ly, ho-ly, ho-ly Lord, God of hosts, e-ter-nal King,
By the heav'ns and earth a-dored; An-gels and arch-an-gels sing,
Chanting ev-er-last-ing-ly, To the blessed Trin-i-ty. A-MEN.

2 Cherubim and seraphim
   Veil their faces with their wings;
Eyes of angels are too dim
   To behold the King of kings,
While they sing eternally
To the blessed Trinity.

3 Alleluia! Lord, to Thee,
   Father, Son, and Holy Ghost,
Three in One, and One in Three,
   Join we with the heavenly host,
Singing everlastingly
To the blessed Trinity. AMEN.

Bishop Wordsworth

99   *The Lord my Shepherd is.*

WILLIAMSON.   S. M.   German.   (Arr. by A. N.)

1. The Lord my Shep-herd is,   I shall be well sup-plied; Since

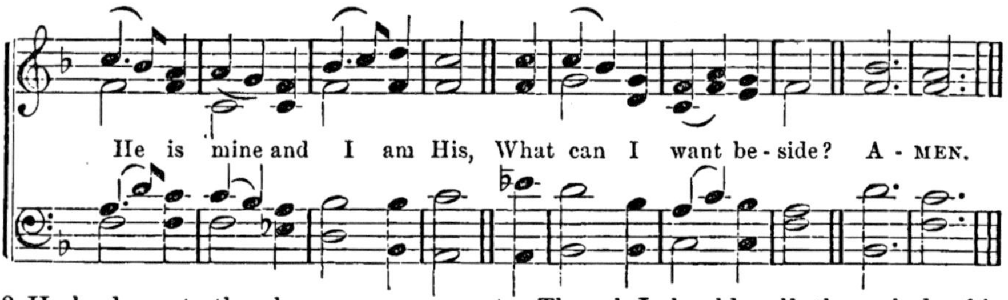

He is mine and I am His, What can I want be-side?   A - MEN.

2 He leads me to the place
    Where heavenly pasture grows,
Where living waters gently pass,
    And full salvation flows.

3 If e'er I go astray,
    He doth my soul reclaim,
And guides me in His own right way,
    For His most holy name.

4 While He affords His aid
    I cannot yield to fear;

Though I should walk through death's
    dark shade,
My Shepherd's with me there.

5 Amid surrounding foes
    Thou dost my table spread ;
My cup with blessings overflows,
    And joy exalts my head.

6 The bounties of Thy love
    Shall crown my foll'wing days,
Nor from Thy house will I remove,
    Nor cease to speak Thy praise. AMEN
                     Dr. Watts.

100   *Lift up your Heads, ye Mighty Gates.*

PRAISE.   L. M.   PRÆTORIUS, 1604.

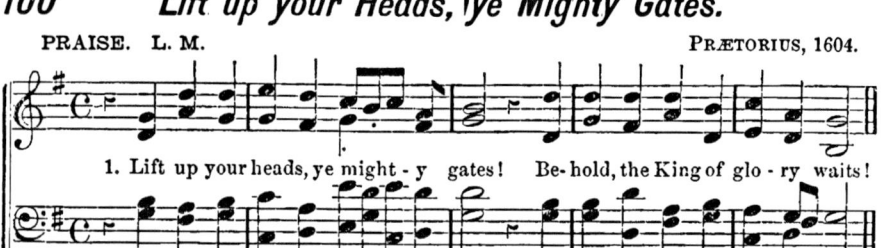

1. Lift up your heads, ye might - y gates! Be - hold, the King of glo - ry waits!

PRAISE.—Continued.

The King of kings is drawing near, The Saviour of the world is here.   A - MEN.

2 Life and salvation doth He bring,
　Wherefore rejoice, and gladly sing;
　Eternal praise, my God, to Thee;
　Creator, wise is Thy decree.

3 Fling wide the portals of your heart,
　Make it a temple, set apart

From earthly use for heaven's employ,
Adorned with prayer and love and joy.

4 Redeemer, come; I open wide
　My heart to Thee; here, Lord, abide;
　Let me Thine inner presence feel,
　Thy grace and love in me reveal. AMEN.

George Weisel, 1635.   Trans. by Cath. Winkworth, 1855.

101　　*Oh for a Thousand Tongues to Sing.*

ST. STEPHEN.　C. M.　　　　　　　　　　　Rev. W. JONES.

1. Oh for a thou-sand tongues to sing   My great Re-deemer's praise!

The glo - ries of my God and King, The tri-umphs of His grace! A - MEN.

2 My gracious Master and my God,
　Assist me to proclaim,
To spread through all the earth abroad
　The honors of Thy name.

3 Jesus! the name that charms our fears,
　That bids our sorrows cease,
'Tis music in the sinner's ears,
　'Tis life and health and peace.

4 He breaks the power of canceled sin,
　He sets the prisoner free,
His blood can make the foulest clean,
　His blood availed for me.

5 Look unto Him, ye nations; own
　Your God, ye fallen race;
Look, and be saved through faith alone,
　Be justified by grace.   AMEN.

Charles Wesley.

102   *Before Jehovah's Awful Throne.*

OLD HUNDRED.   L. M.   W. FRANC.

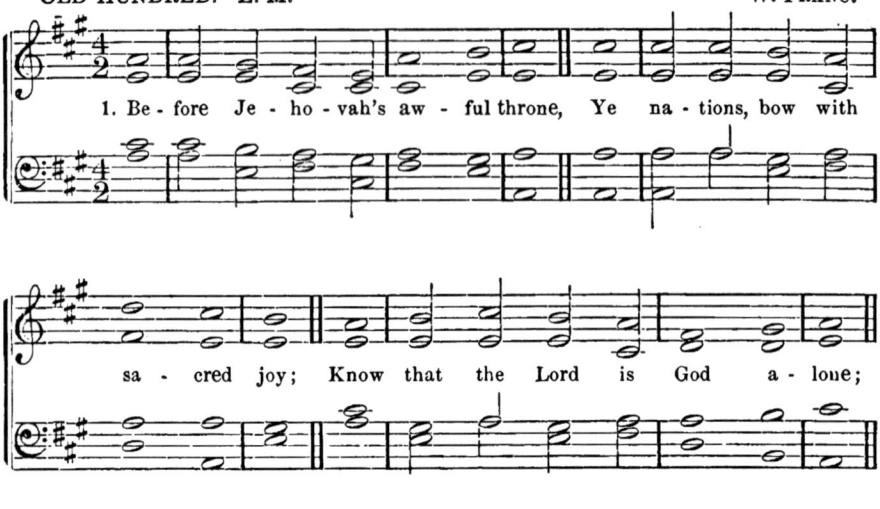

1. Be - fore Je - ho - vah's aw - ful throne, Ye na - tions, bow with

sa - cred joy; Know that the Lord is God a - lone;

He can cre - ate, and He de - stroy. A - MEN.

2 His sovereign power, without our aid,
  Made us of clay and formed us men,
And when, like wandering sheep, we
    strayed,
  He brought us to His fold again.

3 We are His people, we His care,
  Our souls, and all our mortal frame;
What lasting honors shall we rear,
  Almighty Maker, to Thy name?

4 We'll crowd Thy gates with thankful
    songs,
  High as the heavens our voices raise,

And earth, with her ten thousand
    tongues,
  Shall fill Thy courts with sounding
    praise.

5 Wide as the world is Thy command,
  Vast as eternity Thy love;
Firm as a rock Thy truth must
    stand
  When rolling years shall cease to
    move. AMEN.

Dr. Watts.

103   *All Hail the Power of Jesus' Name.*

CORONATION. C. M.   OLIVER HOLDEN.

1. All hail the power of Je-sus' name, Let an-gels pros-trate fall;
Bring forth the roy-al di-a-dem, And crown Him Lord of all,
Bring forth the roy-al di-a-dem, And crown Him Lord of all. A-MEN.

2 Crown Him, ye morning stars of light,
　Who fixed this floating ball ;
Now hail the strength of Israel's might,
　And crown Him Lord of all.

3 Ye chosen seed of Israel's race,
　Ye ransomed from the fall,
Hail Him who saves you by His grace,
　And crown Him Lord of all.

4 Hail Him, ye heirs of David's line,
　Whom David Lord did call,
The God incarnate, Man divine,
　And crown Him Lord of all.

5 Sinners, whose love can ne'er forget
　The wormwood and the gall,
Go spread your trophies at His feet,
　And crown Him Lord of all.

6 Let every kindred, every tribe,
　On this terrestrial ball
To Him all majesty ascribe,
　And crown Him Lord of all.

7 Oh that with yonder sacred throng
　We at His feet may fall ,
We'll join the everlasting song,
　And crown Him Lord of all. AMEN.

Edward Perronet, 1780. Altered.

8

104   *Glorious Things of thee are Spoken.*

AUSTRIA. 8s & 7s. D.   J. HAYDN.

1. Glo - rious things of thee are spo - ken,   Si - on, ci - ty   of   our God; }
He whose word can-not   be   bro - ken   Form'd thee for His own   a - bode. }

On   the   Rock   of   a - ges   found-ed,   What   can shake thy sure re - pose?

With sal - va-tion's walls surrounded, Thou mayst smile at   all   thy foes. A - MEN.

2 See, the streams of living waters,
    Springing from eternal love,
Well supply thy sons and daughters,
    And all fear of want remove;
Who can faint while such a river
    Ever flows their thirst t' assuage,
Grace which, like the Lord, the Giver,
    Never fails from age to age?

3 Round each habitation hovering,
    See the cloud and fire appear,
For a glory and a covering,
    Showing that the Lord is near;
Blest inhabitants of Sion,
    Washed in the Redeemer's blood,
Jesus, whom their souls rely on,
    Makes them kings and priests to God.
                                        AMEN.
                              Rev. F. Newton.

105   *Awake, my Soul! Stretch every Nerve.*

CHRISTMAS. C. M.   HANDEL.

1. A - wake, my soul! stretch ev - 'ry nerve, And press with

vig - or   on ;   A heaven-ly race de - mands thy zeal,

And an im- mor- tal crown, And an im - mor- tal crown. A - MEN.

2 A cloud of witnesses around
  Hold thee in full survey ;
  F orget the steps already trod,
  And onward urge thy way.

3 'Tis God's all-animating voice
  That calls thee from on high,

'Tis His own hand presents the prize
  To thine aspiring eye.

4 Blest Saviour, introduced by Thee,
  Have I my race begun,
  And, crowned with victory, at Thy feet
  I'll lay my laurels down. AMEN.

Dr. Doddridge.

106   *Lord of every Land and Nation.*

PRAISE.   8s & 7s.   ALBERT LOWE.

2 Brightness of the Father's glory,
   Shall Thy praise unutter'd lie?
Shun, my tongue, the guilty silence,
   Sing the Lord who came to die.
      Alleluia, amen!

3 From the highest throne in glory
   To the cross of deepest woe,

All to ransom guilty captives;
   Flow, my praise, for ever flow.
      Alleluia, amen!

4 Come, return, immortal Saviour;
   Come, Lord Jesus, take Thy throne;
Quickly come, and reign for ever,
   Be Thy kingdom all Thine own.
      Alleluia, amen!

107   *Holy Saviour, we Adore Thee.*

SALZBURG.   8s, 7s, & 4.   M. HAYDN.

1. Ho - ly Sa - viour, we a - dore Thee, Seat - ed on the throne of God;

All heav'n's hosts bow down be - fore Thee, And we sing Thy praise a - loud.

Thou art worthy, Thou art worthy! We were ransomed by Thy blood. A - MEN.

2 Saviour, though the world despised
    Thee,
  Though Thou here wast crucified,
  Yet the Father's glory raised Thee,
  Lord of all creation wide;
    Thou art worthy!
  We shall live, for Thou hast died.

3 And though here on earth rejected,
  'Tis but fellowship with Thee;
  What besides could be expected
  Than like Thee, our Lord, to be?

Thou art worthy!
Thou from earth hast set us free.

4 Haste the day of Thy returning,
  With Thy ransomed Church to
    reign;
  Then shall end our days of mourning,
  We shall sing with rapture then,
    "Thou art worthy!"
Come, Lord Jesus, come. Amen.
            AMEN.

Samuel P. Tregelles.

108   *I Love Thy Kingdom, Lord.*

SILVER STREET. S. M.   I. SMITH.

1. I love Thy kingdom, Lord, The house of Thine a - bode, The Church our

blest Re - deem - er saved With His own pre - cious blood. A - MEN.

2 I love Thy Church, O God,
  Her walls before Thee stand
Dear as the apple of Thine eye,
  And graven on Thy hand.

3 For her my tears shall fall,
  For her my prayers ascend,
To her my cares and toils be given
  Till toils and cares shall end.

4 Beyond my highest joy
  I prize her heavenly ways,

Her sweet communion, solemn vows,
  Her hymns of love and praise.

5 Jesus, Thou Friend divine,
  Our Saviour and our King,
Thy hand from every snare and foe
  Shall great deliverance bring.

6 Sure as Thy truth shall last,
  To Sion shall be given
The brightest glories earth can yield,
  And brighter bliss of heaven. AMEN.
                                 Dr. Dwight.

109   *Round the Lord in Glory Seated.*

COBLENTZ. 8s & 7s. D.   German. (Arr. by A. NEVIN.)

1. Round the Lord in glo - ry seat - ed, Cher - u - bim and ser - a - phim ⎫
Filled His tem - ple, and re - peat - ed Each to each th' al - ter-nate hymn. ⎭

D.C. Un - to Thee be glo - ry giv - en, Ho-ly, ho - ly, ho - ly Lord!"

COBLENTZ.—Continued.

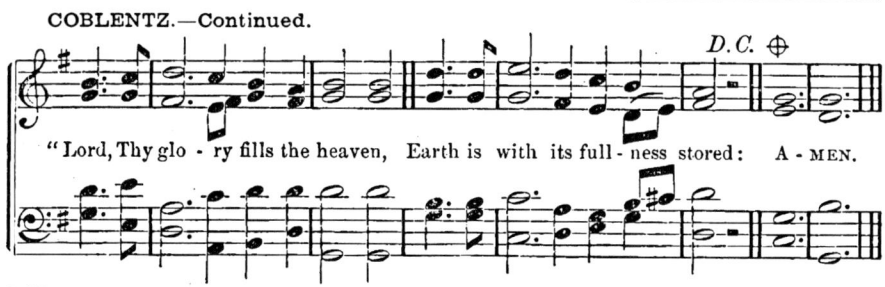

"Lord, Thy glo - ry fills the heaven, Earth is with its full - ness stored: A - MEN.

2 Heaven is still with glory ringing,
  Earth takes up the angels' cry,
"Holy, holy, holy," singing,
"Lord of hosts, the Lord most high!
Lord, Thy glory fills the heaven,
  Earth is with its fullness stored,
Unto Thee be glory given,
  Holy, holy, holy Lord!"

3 With His seraph-train before Him,
  With His holy Church below,
Thus conspire we to adore Him,
  Bid we thus our anthem flow:
"Lord, Thy glory fills the heaven,
  Earth is with its fullness stored,
Unto Thee be glory given,
  Holy, holy, holy Lord!" AMEN.
Richard Mant.

110 Come, We that Love the Lord.

CAMBRIDGE. S. M. REV. R. HARRISON.

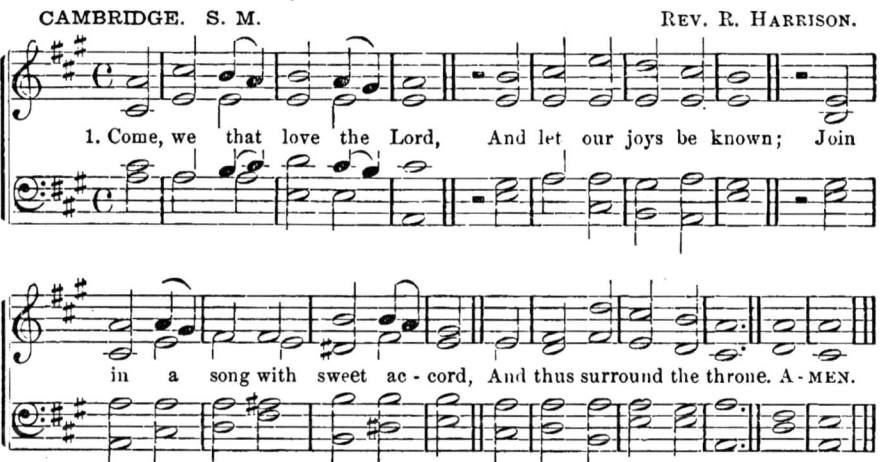

1. Come, we that love the Lord, And let our joys be known; Join
in a song with sweet ac - cord, And thus surround the throne. A - MEN.

2 Let those refuse to sing
  That never knew our God,
But favorites of the heavenly King
  May speak their joys abroad.

3 The men of grace have found
  Glory begun below;

Celestial fruits on earthly ground
  From faith and hope may grow.

4 Then let our songs abound,
  And every tear be dry;
We're marching through Immanuel's
  ground,
To fairer worlds on high. AMEN.
Isaac Watts, 1707.

111   *Songs of Praise the Angels Sang.*

CLARION. 7s.

E. F. RIMBAULT.

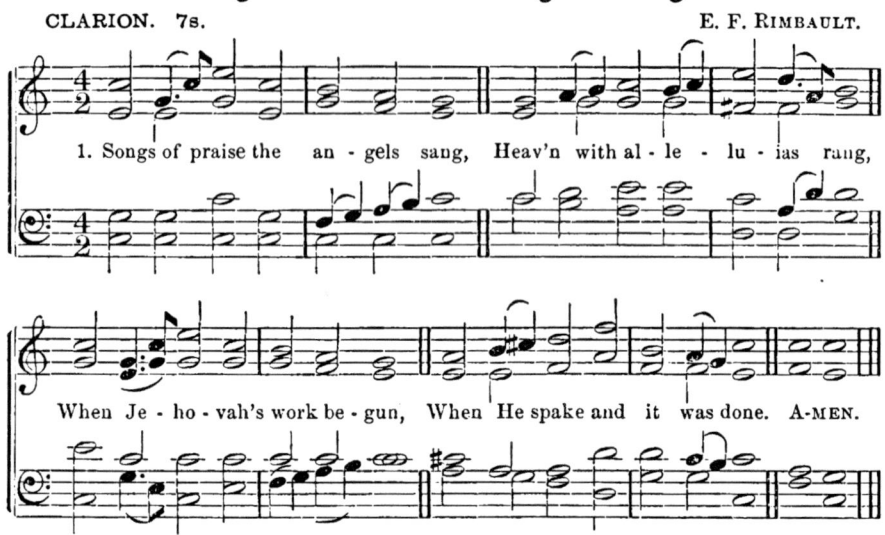

1. Songs of praise the an - gels sang, Heav'n with al - le - lu - ias rang,

When Je - ho - vah's work be - gun, When He spake and it was done. A-MEN.

2 Songs of praise awoke the morn
When the Prince of peace was born,
Songs of praise arose when He
Captive led captivity.

3 Heaven and earth must pass away,
Songs of praise shall crown that day;
God will make new heavens and earth,
Songs of praise shall hail their birth.

4 And shall man alone be dumb
Till that glorious kingdom come?

No; the Church delights to raise
Psalms and hymns and songs of praise.

5 Saints below, with heart and voice,
Still in songs of praise rejoice,
Learning here, by faith and love,
Songs of praise to sing above.

6 Borne upon their latest breath,
Songs of praise shall conquer death;
Then, amidst eternal joy,
Songs of praise their powers employ.

AMEN.

J. Montgomery.

112   *Far Beyond all Comprehension.*

WINSLOW. 8s & 7s.

ANON.

1. Far be - yond all com-pre - hen - sion Is Je - ho - vah's cov'nant love;

WINSLOW.—Continued.

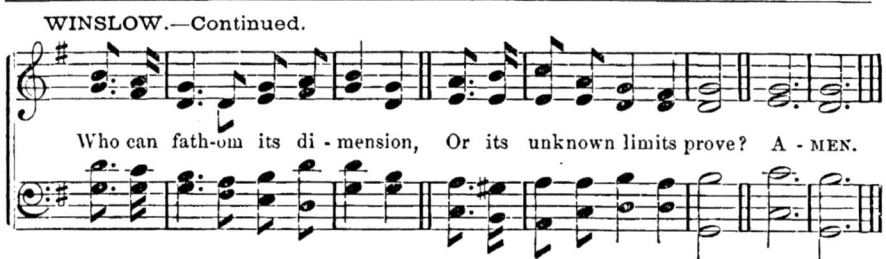

Who can fath-om its di-mension, Or its unknown limits prove? A-MEN.

2 Ere the earth upon its basis
　By creating power was built,
His designs were wise and gracious
　For removing human guilt.

3 He displayed his grand intention
　On the Mount of Calvary
When He died for our redemption,
　Lifted high upon the tree.

4 Oh how sweet to view the flowing
　Of His soul-redeeming blood,
With divine assurance knowing
　That it made my peace with God!

5 Freely Thou wilt bring to heaven
　All Thy chosen ransomed race,
Who to Thee, their Head, were given
　In the covenant of grace. AMEN.

113　　*Children of the Heavenly King.*

PLEYEL'S HYMN. 7s.　　　　　　　　　　　　　　PLEYEL.

1. Chil-dren of the heavenly King, As we jour-ney, sweet-ly sing;

Sing your Saviour's worthy praise, Glorious in His works and ways. A-MEN.

2 We are traveling home to God
In the way the fathers trod;
They are happy now, and we
Soon their happiness shall see.

3 Banished once, by sin betrayed,
Christ our Advocate was made;

Pardoned now, no more we roam;
Christ conducts us to our home.

4 Lord, obediently we go,
Gladly leaving all below;
Only Thou our Leader be,
And we still will follow Thee. AMEN.
John Cennick.

114   ## Praise the Lord of Heaven.

ST. MARK.   6s & 5s. D.   ANON.

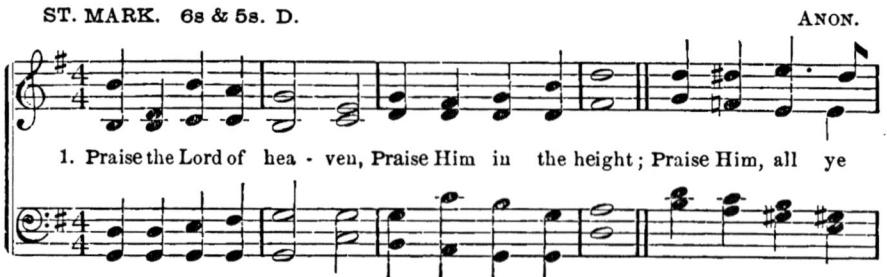

1. Praise the Lord of hea - ven, Praise Him in the height; Praise Him, all ye

angels, Praise Him, stars and light; Praise Him, clouds and waters, Which above the skies,

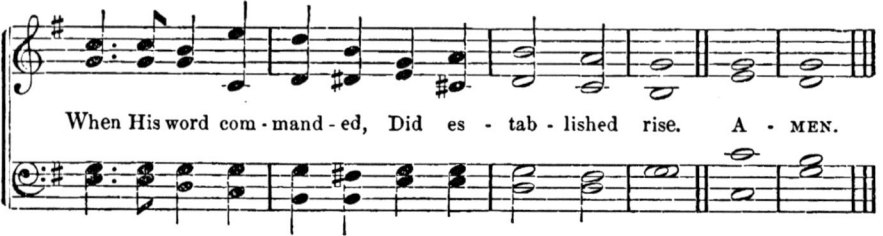

When His word com - mand - ed, Did es - tab - lished rise.   A - MEN.

2 Praise the Lord, ye fountains
   Of the deeps and seas,
Rocks and hills and mountains,
   Cedars, and all trees;
Praise Him, clouds and vapors,
   Snow and hail and fire,
Stormy wind, fulfilling
   Only His desire.

3 Praise Him, fowls and cattle,
   Princes and all kings;
Praise Him, men and maidens
   All created things;
For the name of God is
   Excellent alone,
Over earth His footstool,
   Over heaven His throne. AMEN.

115 *Now thank we all our God.*

NUN DANKET ALLE GOTT. P. M.

F. CRÜGER.

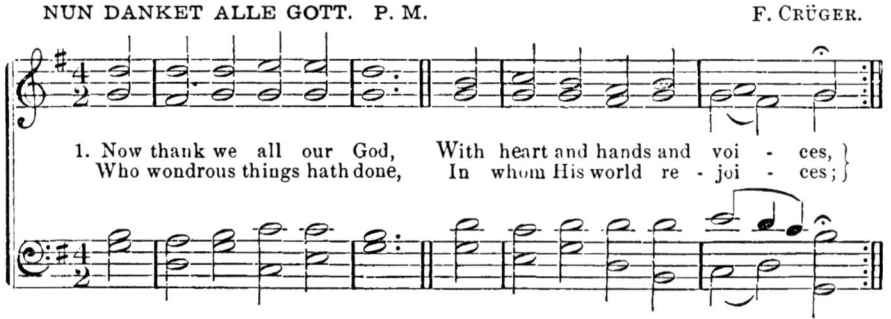

1. Now thank we all our God, With heart and hands and voi - ces,
Who wondrous things hath done, In whom His world re - joi - ces;

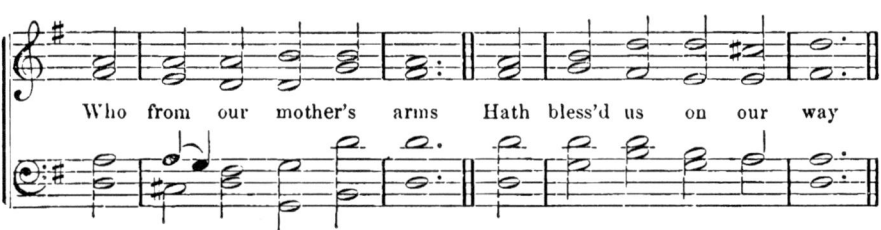

Who from our mother's arms Hath bless'd us on our way

With countless gifts of love, And still is ours to - day. A - MEN.

2 Oh may this bounteous God
Through all our life be near us,
With ever-joyful hearts
And blessed peace to cheer us,
And keep us in His grace,
And guide us when perplexed,
And free us from all ills
In this world and the next.

3 All praise and thanks to God
The Father now be given,
The Son and Him who reigns
With them in highest heaven,
The one eternal God,
Whom earth and heaven adore,
For thus it was, is now,
And shall be evermore. AMEN.

Tr. Miss C. Winckworth.

116　　*Beautiful Saviour, King of Creation.*

CRUSADER'S HYMN. P. M.　　　　　　　　　　　ANON.

1. Beau - ti - ful Sa - viour, King of cre - a - tion, Son of God and Son of man! Tru - ly I'd love Thee, Tru - ly I'd serve Thee, Light of my soul, my Joy, my Crown. A - MEN.

2 Fair are the meadows,
　Fairer the woodlands,
Robed in flowers of blooming spring;
　Jesus is fairer,
　Jesus is purer,
He makes our sorrowing spirits sing.

3 Fair is the sunshine,
　Fairer the moonlight,
And the sparkling stars on high;

Jesus shines brighter,
Jesus shines purer,
Than all the angels in the sky.

4 Beautiful Saviour,
　Lord of the nations,
Son of God and Son of man!
　Glory and honor,
　Praise, adoration,
Now and for evermore be Thine. AMEN.

117   *Hark! that glorious Burst of Praise.*

THANKSGIVING.   7s.   6 lines.   W. B. GILBERT.

Hark! that glorious burst of praise Which the ransomed le - gions raise,

While the ceaseless waves of song Sweep their gold - en harps a - long

In a full tri-umph-ant strain—"To the Lamb for sin - ners slain!" A - MEN.

2 Grant us, Lord, to hear that sound
Swell Thy golden city round,
And, while absent far away

In this prison-house of clay,
Let our souls take up the psalm
"Worthy, worthy is the Lamb!" AMEN.

118   *Salvation! oh the Joyful Sound.*

ASHLEY. C. M.   Dr. MADEN.

1. Sal - va - tion! oh the joy - ful sound, Glad tid - ings
to our ears, A sov'-reign balm for ev'-ry wound, A
cor - dial for our fears.   Glo-ry, hon-or, praise, and power Be un-to the
Lamb for ev - er! Je - sus Christ is our Re-deem-er; Al - le - lu - ia,

ASHLEY.—Continued.

Al - le - lu - ia, Al - le - lu - ia, praise the Lord! A - MEN.

2 Buried in sorrow and in sin,
   At hell's dark door we lay,
   But we arise by grace divine
   To see a heavenly day.—*Cho.*

3 Salvation! let the echo fly
   The spacious earth around,

While all the armies of the sky
Conspire to raise the sound.—*Cho.*

4 Salvation! O Thou bleeding Lamb,
   To Thee the praise belongs;
   Our hearts shall kindle at Thy name,
   Thy name inspire our songs.—*Cho.*

AMEN. *Dr. Watts.*

119   *To Christ, the Prince of Peace.*

BARRINGTON. S. M.   JOHN GAUNT.

1. To Christ, the Prince of peace, And Son of God, we sing;

To Him who saved us by His love, Let ho - ly anthems ring. A - MEN.

2 Deep in His heart for us
   The wound of love He bore
   That love which still He kindles in
   The hearts that Him adore.

3 O Jesus! Victim blest!
   What else but love divine

Could Thee constrain to open thus
That sacred heart of Thine?

4 Hide me in Thy dear heart,
   For thither do I fly;   [death
   There seek Thy grace through life; in
   Thine immortality. AMEN.

Latin Hymn. Translated by E. Caswall.

120 *Jesu, Meek and Gentle.*

ST. LUCIAN. 6s & 5s. C. H. RINCK.

1. Je - su, meek and gen - tle, Son of God Most High,

Pitying, lov - ing Sa - viour, Hear Thy children's cry. A - MEN.

2 Pardon our offences,
    Loose our captive chains,
  Break down every idol
    Which our soul detain

3 Give us holy freedom,
    Fill our hearts with love,
  Draw us, Holy Jesu,
    To the realms above.

4 Lead us on our journey,
    Be Thyself the way
  Through terrestrial darkness
    To celestial day.

5 Jesu, meek and gentle,
    Son of God most high,
  Pitying, loving Saviour,
    Hear Thy children's cry. AMEN.
      Rev. G. R. Prynne.

121 *Thou art the Way; to Thee Alone.*

MARLOW. C. M. Arr. by LOWELL MASON.

1. Thou art the Way; to Thee a - lone From sin and death we flee;

MARLOW.—Continued.

And he who would the Father seek Must seek Him, Lord, by Thee. A - MEN.

2 Thou art the Truth; Thy word alone
  True wisdom can impart;
  Thou only canst instruct the mind
  And purify the heart.

3 Thou art the Life; the rending tomb
  Proclaims Thy conquering arm,

And those who put their trust in Thee
  Nor death nor hell shall harm.

4 Thou art the Way, the Truth, the Life;
  Grant us that Way to know,
  That Truth to keep, that Life to win.
  Whose joys eternal flow. AMEN.

Bishop Doane.

122 *Jesus, Thy boundless Love to me.*

MISSIONARY CHANT. L. M.   ZEUNER.

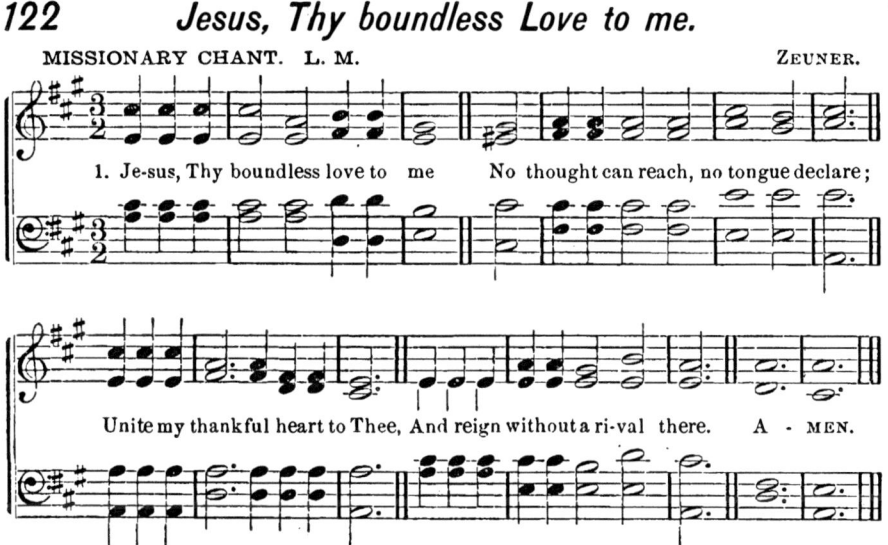

1. Je-sus, Thy boundless love to me   No thought can reach, no tongue declare;

Unite my thankful heart to Thee, And reign without a ri-val there. A - MEN.

2 Thy love, how cheering is its ray!
  All pain before its presence flies;
  Care, anguish, sorrow melt away
  Where'er its healing beams arise.

3 Oh let Thy love my soul inflame,
  And to Thy service sweetly bind;

Transfuse it through my inmost frame,
  And mould me wholly to Thy mind.

4 Thy love, in sufferings, be my peace,
  Thy love, in weakness, make me strong,
  And when the storms of life shall cease,
  Thy love shall be in heaven my song.
  AMEN.

Paul Gerhart, 1659. Trans. by John Wesley, 1739. Altered.

123   *Lord, as to Thy dear Cross we Flee.*

ST. PETERS. C. M.   A. R. REINAGLE.

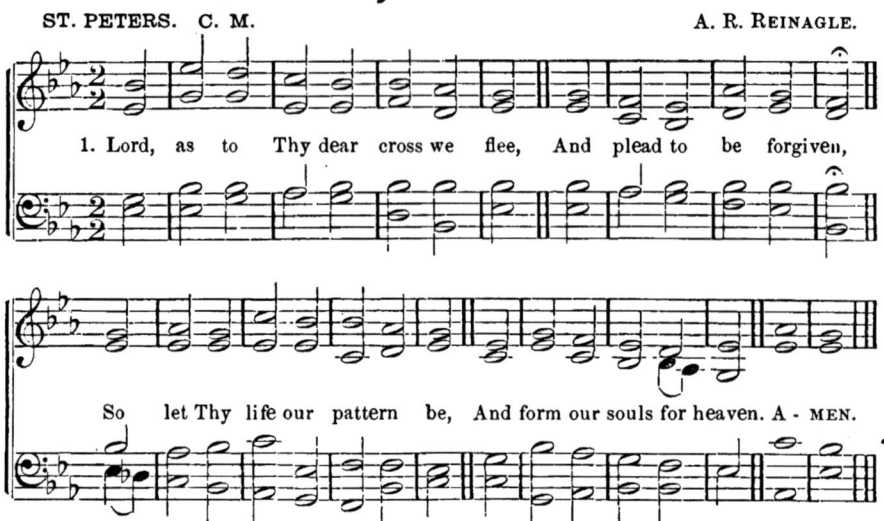

1. Lord, as to Thy dear cross we flee, And plead to be forgiven,

So let Thy life our pattern be, And form our souls for heaven. A - MEN.

2 Help us, through good report and ill,
    Our daily cross to bear,
Like Thee to do our Father's will,
    Our brethren's griefs to share.

3 Let grace our selfishness expel,
    Our earthliness refine,
And kindness in our bosoms dwell
    As free and true as Thine.

4 If joy shall at Thy bidding fly,
    And grief's dark day come on,

We, in our turn, would meekly cry,
    "Father, Thy will be done."

5 Should friends misjudge or foes defame,
    Or brethren faithless prove,
Then, like Thine own, be all our aim
    To conquer them by love.

6 Kept peaceful in the midst of strife,
    Forgiving and forgiven,
Oh may we lead the pilgrim's life,
    And follow Thee to heaven. AMEN.

         John Hampden Gurney, 1838.

124   *A Charge to Keep I have.*

DOVER. S. M.   A. WILLIAMS.

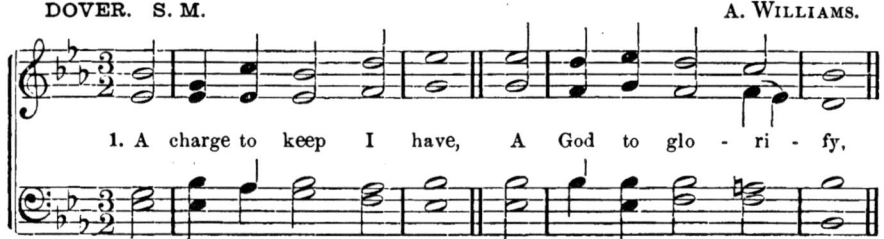

1. A charge to keep I have, A God to glo - ri - fy,

DOVER—Continued.

A nev-er-dy-ing soul to save, And fit it for the sky. A-MEN.

2 To serve the present age,
　My calling to fulfill,
Oh, may it all my powers engage
　To do my Master's will.

3 Arm me with jealous care,
　As in Thy sight to live,

And oh, Thy servant, Lord, prepare
　A strict account to give.

4 Help me to watch and pray,
　And on Thyself rely,
Assured, if I my trust betray,
　I shall for ever die. AMEN.

Rev. C. Wesley.

125　Father, 'tis Thine each Day to Yield.

ST. AGNES.　C. M.　　　　　　　　　　　　Rev. Dr. DYKES.

1. Fa-ther, 'tis Thine each day to yield Our wants a fresh sup-ply,

Thou cloth'st the lilies of the field, And hear'st the ra-vens cry: A-MEN.

2 Thy love in all Thy works we see,
　Thy promise, Lord, we plead,
And humbly cast our care on Thee,
　Who knowest all our need.

3 Let not the world engage our love,
　Nor cares our bosoms fill,

But fix our hearts on things above,
　That we may do Thy will.

4 The comfort of Thy light bestow,
　Our faith and hope increase,
And let us in Thy presence know
　Contentment, joy, and peace. AMEN.

Edward Osler.

126   *O Jesus, Saviour of the Lost.*

MARTYRDOM.   C. M.   H. WILSON.

1. O Je - sus, Sa - viour of the lost, My Rock and

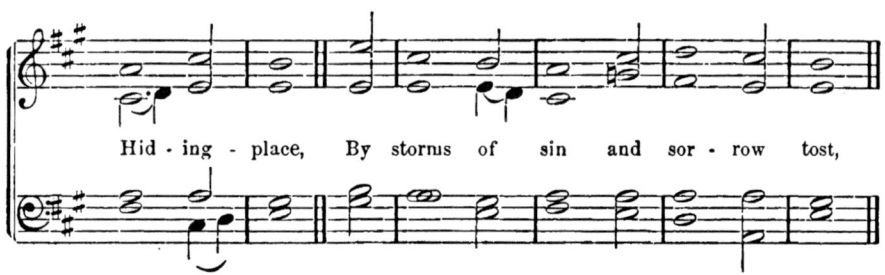

Hid - ing - place, By storms of sin and sor - row tost,

I seek Thy shel - t'ring grace.   A - - MEN.

2 Guilty, "Forgive me, Lord!" I cry ;
  Pursued by foes, I come ;
  A sinner, save me, or I die ;   •
  An outcast, take me home.

3 Once safe in Thine almighty arms,
  Let storms come on amain ;

There danger never, never harms,
  There death itself is gain.

4 And when I stand before Thy throne
  And all Thy glory see,
Still be my righteousness alone
  To hide myself in Thee.   AMEN.

Edward H. Bickersteth, 1858.

127 *Abide among us with Thy Grace.*

MEDFIELD. C. M. W. MATHER.

1. A - bide a - mong us with Thy grace, Lord Je - sus, ev - er - more, Nor let us e'er to sin give place, Nor grieve Him we a - dore. A - MEN.

2 Abide among us with Thy word,
   Redeemer whom we love;
Thy help and mercy here afford,
   And life with Thee above.

3 Abide among us with Thy ray,
   O Light that lighten'st all,
And let Thy truth preserve our way,
   Nor suffer us to fall.

4 Abide with us to bless us still,
   O bounteous Lord of peace;

With grace and power our souls fulfill,
   Our faith and love increase.

5 Abide among us as our Shield,
   O Captain of Thy host,
That to the world we may not yield,
   Nor e'er forsake our post.

6 Abide with us in faithful love,
   Our God and Saviour be;
Thy help at need oh let us prove,
   And keep us true to Thee. AMEN.

J. Stagmann. Trans. by Catherine Winckworth.

128   *Mercy, O Thou Son of David.*

BARTIMEUS.   8s & 7s.   STEPHEN JENKS.

1. "Mer - cy, O Thou Son of Da-vid!" Thus the blind Bar - tim - eus prayed;

"Oth - ers by Thy word are savèd; Now to me af - ford Thine aid." A - MEN.

2 Many for his crying chid him,
     But he called the louder still,
Till the gracious Saviour bid him,
     "Come and ask me what you will."

3 Money was not what he wanted,
     Though by begging used to live,
But he asked, and Jesus granted,
     Alms which none but He could give:

4 "Lord, remove this grievous blindness,
     Let my eyes behold the day;"

Straight he saw, and, won by kindness,
     Followed Jesus in the way.

5 Oh methinks I hear him praising,
     Publishing to all around,
"Friends, is not my case amazing?
     What a Saviour I have found!

6 Oh that all the blind but knew Him,
     And would be advised by me!
Surely they would hasten to Him,
     He would cause them all to see."
                           AMEN.
                           Newton.

129   *Father of Eternal Grace.*

THEODORA.   7s.   From HANDEL.

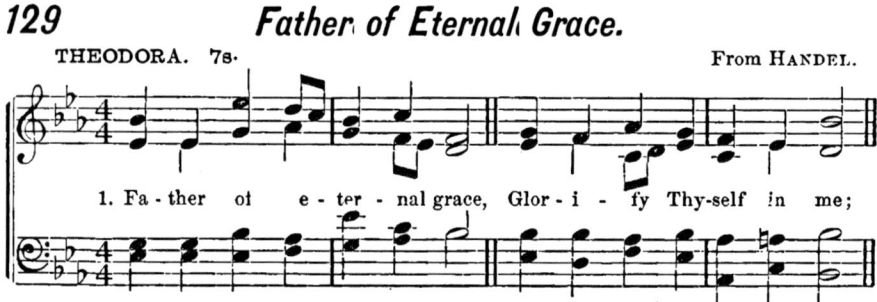

1. Fa - ther of e - ter - nal grace, Glor - i - fy Thy-self in me;

THEODORA.—Continued.

Meek-ly beaming in my face   May the world Thine image see.   A - MEN.

2 Happy only in Thy love,
  Poor, unfriended, or unknown,
  Fix my thoughts on things above,
  Stay my heart on Thee alone.

3 Humble, holy, all-resigned
  To Thy will—Thy will be done—

Give me, Lord, the perfect mind
Of Thy well-beloved Son.

4 Counting gain and glory loss,
  May I tread the path He trod,
  Die with Jesus on the cross,
  Rise with Him to Thee, my God. AMEN.

James Montgomery, 1808.

130   *Jesus, I Live to Thee.*

MORNINGTON. S. M.   LORD MORNINGTON.

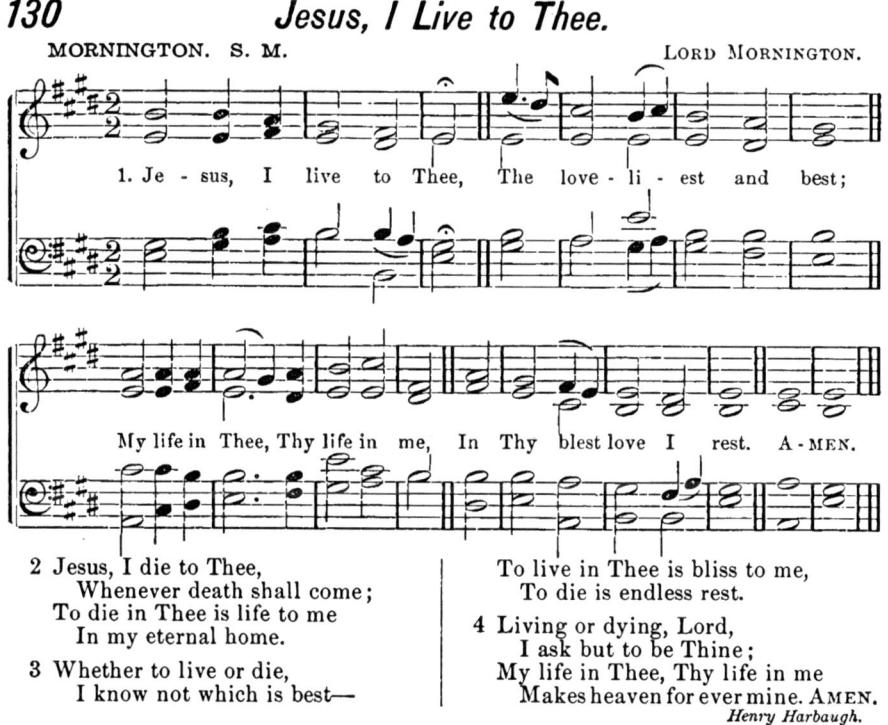

1. Je - sus,   I   live   to Thee,   The love - li - est   and   best;

My life in Thee, Thy life in   me,   In   Thy blest love   I   rest. A - MEN.

2 Jesus, I die to Thee,
  Whenever death shall come;
  To die in Thee is life to me
  In my eternal home.

3 Whether to live or die,
  I know not which is best—

To live in Thee is bliss to me,
To die is endless rest.

4 Living or dying, Lord,
  I ask but to be Thine;
  My life in Thee, Thy life in me
  Makes heaven for ever mine. AMEN.

Henry Harbaugh.

131 *Jesu, my Lord, my God, my All.*

S. FINBAR. 8s.   ANONYMOUS.

1. Je - su, my Lord, my God, my All,   Hear me, blest Sa - viour,
when   I   call;   Hear me, and   from   Thy   dwell - ing - place
Pour down the rich - es   of   Thy grace.   Je - su,   my Lord,   I
Thee a - dore;   Oh make me love Thee more and more.   A - MEN.

2 Jesu, too late I Thee have sought;
How can I love Thee as I ought,
And how extol Thy matchless fame,
The glorious beauty of Thy name?
Jesu, my Lord, I Thee adore;
Oh make me love Thee more and more.

3 Jesu, what didst Thou find in me
That Thou hast dealt so lovingly?
How great the joy that Thou hast
brought,
So far exceeding hope or thought!

Jesu, my Lord, I Thee adore;
Oh make me love Thee more and more.

4 Jesu, of Thee shall be my song,
To Thee my heart and soul belong;
All that I have or am is Thine,
And Thou, blest Saviour, Thou art
mine.
Jesu, my Lord, I Thee adore;
Oh make me love Thee more and more.
AMEN.

132 Who is there like Thee?

GERMAN CHORAL. Seelenbrautigam. Arr. by H. S.

1. Who is there like Thee, Je-sus, un-to me? None are like Thee,
D.C. None on earth have we, None in heaven, like Thee.

none a-bove Thee, Thou art al-to-geth-er love-ly. A-MEN.

2 Love that warmly glowed,
Blood that freely flowed,
Life that stooped to death to save me,
And a deathless being gave me,
Bore my guilty load,
Brought me back to God,

3 Plant Thyself in me;
I will learn of Thee
To be holy, meek, and tender,
Wrath and pride and self surrender;

Nothing shouldst Thou see
But Thyself in me.

4 When on death's cold strand
I one day shall stand,
Let Thy presence go beside me,
Through the gloomy waters guide me;
Grant me then to stand,
Lord, at Thy right hand.
AMEN.

133 - *Guide me, O Thou great Jehovah !*

AUTUMN. 8s & 7s. D.   SPANISH MELODY.

1. Guide me, O Thou great Je-ho - vah! Pilgrim through this barren land;

I am weak, but Thou art mighty, Hold me with Thy powerful hand:
D.S. Bread of heaven, Bread of heaven, Feed me till I want no more.

Bread of heaven, Bread of heaven, Feed me till I want no more, A - MEN.

2 Open now the crystal fountain
  Whence the healing streams do flow,
Let the fiery, cloudy pillar
  Lead me all my journey through ;
    Strong Deliv'rer,
  Be Thou still my strength and shield.

3 When I tread the verge of Jordan,
  Bid my anxious fears subside ;
Death of death, and hell's destruction,
  Land me safe on Canaan's side ;
    Songs of praises
  I will ever give to Thee. AMEN.

W. Williams.

134 *Saviour, like a Shepherd lead us.*

SHEPHERD. 8s, 7s, & 4. BRADBURY.

1. Saviour, like a shepherd lead us; Much we need Thy tend'rest care;
In Thy pleasant pastures feed us, For our use Thy folds pre pare.

Bless-ed Je - sus, Bless-ed Je - sus, Thou hast bought us, Thine we are,

Blessed Je - sus, Blessed Je - sus, Thou hast bought us, Thine we are. A - MEN.

2 Thou hast promised to receive us,
  Poor and sinful though we be;
Thou hast mercy to relieve us,
  Grace to cleanse, and power to free.
  ‖: Blessed Jesus,
  Let us early turn to Thee. :‖

3 Early let us seek Thy favor,
  Early let us do Thy will;
Blessed Lord and only Saviour,
  With Thy love our bosoms fill.
  ‖: Blessed Jesus,
  Thou hast loved us, love us still. :‖
            AMEN.

135　Jesus, I my Cross have taken.

NETTLETON.　8s & 7s. D.　　　　　　　　　　　ANON.

1. Je-sus, I my cross have ta-ken, All to leave and follow Thee;
Des-ti-tute, de-spised, for-sa-ken, Thou from hence my all shalt be.

D.C. Yet how rich is my con-di-tion! God and heaven are still my own.

Per-ish every fond am-bi-tion, All I've sought or hoped or known; A-MEN.

D.C. ⊕

2 Go, then, earthly fame and treasure!
　Come, disaster, scorn, and pain!
In Thy service pain is pleasure,
　With Thy favor loss is gain.
I have called Thee, Abba Father,
　I have stayed my heart on Thee;
Storms may howl and clouds may
　　gather:
　All must work for good to me.

3 Man may trouble and distress me,
　'Twill but drive me to Thy breast;
Life with trials hard may press me,
　Heaven will bring me sweeter rest.

Oh 'tis not in grief to harm me
　While Thy love is left to me,
Oh 'twere not in joy to charm me
　Were that joy unmixed with Thee.

4 Take, my soul, thy full salvation,
　Rise o'er sin and fear and care,
Joy to find, in every station,
　Something still to do or bear.
Haste thee on from grace to glory,
　Armed by faith and winged by prayer;
Heaven's eternal day's before thee,
　God's own hand shall guide thee there.

Henry Francis Lyte, 1833.

136　To Him who Children Blest.

REST. S. M.　　　　　　　　　　　　SIR JOHN GOSS.

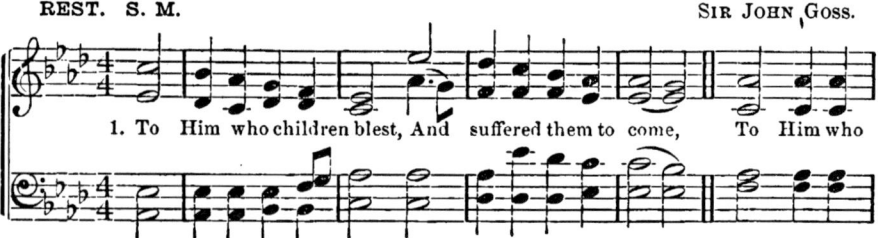

1. To Him who children blest, And suffered them to come, To Him who

REST.—Continued.

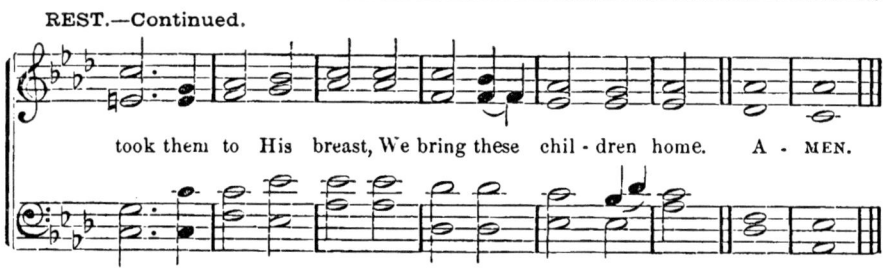

took them to His breast, We bring these chil - dren home. A - MEN.

2 To Thee, O God, whose face
　Their angels always see,
　We bring them, praying that Thy grace
　May bind their souls to Thee.

3 And as this water falls
　On each unconscious brow,
　Lord, let Thy Holy Spirit seal
　The sacramental vow. AMEN.

137   *Soldiers of Christ, Arise.*

ST. LUKE. S. M.   Dr. RANDALL.

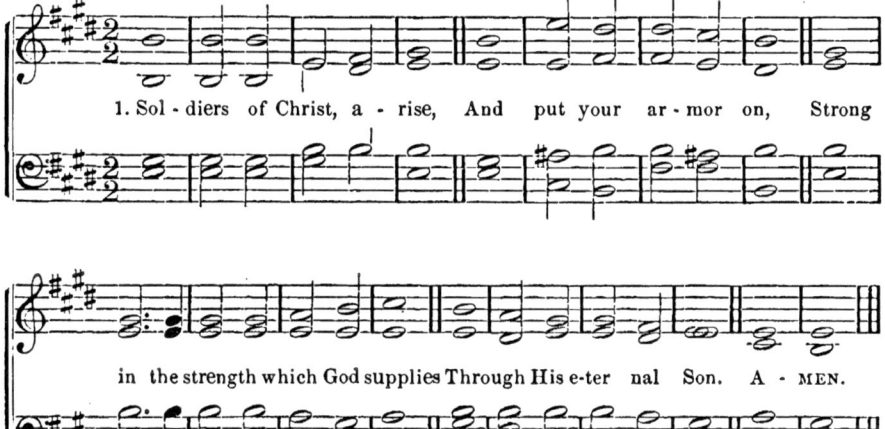

1. Sol - diers of Christ, a - rise, And put your ar - mor on, Strong

in the strength which God supplies Through His e-ter nal Son. A - MEN.

2 Strong in the Lord of hosts,
　And in His mighty power,
　Who in the strength of Jesus trusts,
　Is more than conqueror.

3 Stand, then, in His great might,
　With all His strength endued,

And take to arm you for the fight
　The panoply of God;

4 That, having all things done,
　And all your conflicts past,
　You may o'ercome through Christ alone,
　And stand complete at last. AMEN.

C. Wesley.

138   *Jerusalem the Golden.*

EWING. 7s & 6s. D.   ALEXANDER EWING.

1. Je - ru - sa - lem the gold - en, With milk and hon - ey blest,

Be - neath Thy con - tem - pla - tion Sink heart and voice op - prest.

I know not, oh I know not, What joys a - wait us there,

What ra - dian - cy of glo - ry, What bliss be - yond compare. A - MEN.

2 They stand, those halls of Sion,
　All jubilant with song,
And bright with many an angel,
　And all the martyr-throng;
The Prince is ever in them,
　The daylight is serene,
The pastures of the blessed
　Are decked in glorious sheen.

3 There is the throne of David,
　And there, from care released,
The shout of them that triumph,
　The song of them that feast,
And they who with their Leader
　Have conquered in the fight
For ever and for ever
　Are clad in robes of white. AMEN.

St. Bernard. Tr. by Neale.

139 *Angels of Jesus.*

ANGELICA. 11s, 10s, & 9.　　　　　Arr. by J. M. ARMSTRONG.

1. Hark, hark, my soul! An - gel - ic songs are swelling O'er earth's green fields and
o-ceau's wave-beat shore: How sweet the truth those blessed strains are tell - ing

CHORUS.

Of that new life when sin shall be no more! An - gels of Je - sus,

ANGELICA.—Continued.

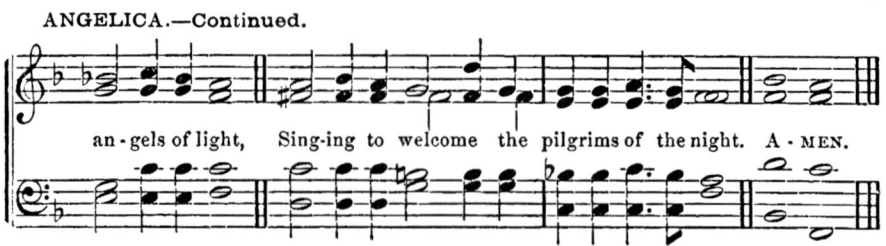

an - gels of light,   Sing-ing to welcome   the pilgrims of the night. A - MEN.

2 Onward we go, for still we hear them singing,
  "Come, weary souls, for Jesus bids you come,"
And, through the dark its echoes sweetly ringing,
  The music of the gospel leads us home.
        Angels of Jesus, etc.

3 Far, far away, like bells at evening pealing,
  The voice of Jesus sounds o'er land and sea,
And laden souls by thousands meekly stealing,
  Kind Shepherd, turn their weary steps to Thee.
        Angels of Jesus, etc.

4 Rest comes at length, though life be long and dreary;
  The day must dawn, and darksome night be past;
All journeys end in welcome to the weary,
  And heaven, the heart's true home, will come at last.
        Angels of Jesus, etc.

5 Angels, sing on, your faithful watches keeping;
  Sing us sweet fragments of the songs above,
Till morning's joy shall end the night of weeping,
  And life's long shadows break in cloudless love.
        Angels of Jesus, etc. AMEN.

                                    Rev. H. W. Faber.

140   *O Mother dear, Jerusalem.*

JERUSALEM. C. M.   TRADITIONAL.

1. O   moth-er   dear, Je - ru - sa - lem, When shall I come to Thee? When

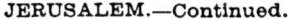

JERUSALEM.—Continued.

shall my sor-rows have an end, Thy joys when shall I see?

2 Jerusalem the city is
  Of God our King alone;
The Lamb of God, its light and bliss,
  Sits on His glorious throne.

3 O happy harbor of God's saints,
  O sweet and pleasant soil!
In thee no sorrow may be found,
  No grief, no care, no toil.

4 No dimming clouds o'ershadow thee,
  No dull nor darksome night,
But every soul shines as the sun,
  For God Himself gives light.

5 Jerusalem, God's dwelling-place,
  I love and long to see;
Oh that my sorrows had an end,
  That I might dwell in thee.

6 Thy walls are made of precious stones,
  Thy bulwarks diamond-square,
Thy gates are made of Orient-pearl;
  O God! if I were there,

7 With cherubim and seraphim,
  And holy souls of men,
To sing thy praise, O God of hosts,
  For ever, and amen.

Francis Baker, 1616. Altered by David Dickson, 1649.

141   *Second Tune.*

MONACA. C. M.   E. A.

1. O mo-ther dear, Je-ru-sa-lem, When shall I come to Thee?

When shall my sor-rows have an end, Thy joys when shall I see? A-MEN.

10

142   *O Paradise, O Paradise!*

HOPKINS. P. M.   HENRY SMART.

1. O Par - a - dise, O Par - a - dise! Who doth not crave for rest?

Who would not seek the hap - py land Where they that loved are blest—

CHORUS.

Where loy - al hearts and true Stand ev - er in the light,

All rapture through and through, In God's most ho - ly sight? A - MEN.

2 O Paradise, O Paradise!
  The world is growing old;
Who would not be at rest and free
  Where love is never cold?—*Cho.*

3 O Paradise, O Paradise!
  'Tis weary waiting here;
I long to be where Jesus is,
  To feel, to see Him near.—*Cho.*

4 O Paradise, O Paradise!
  I want to sin no more;

I want to be as pure on earth
  As on thy spotless shore.—*Cho.*

5 O Paradise, O Paradise!
  I greatly long to see
The special place my dearest Lord
  In love prepares for me.—*Cho.*

6 Lord Jesus, King of Paradise,
  Oh keep me in Thy love,
And guide me to that happy land
  Of perfect rest above.—*Cho.* AMEN.

Rev. F. W. Faber.

143   *For Ever with the Lord.*

FAITH. S. M.   DEAN ALDRICH.

1. "For ev - er with the Lord!" A - men, so let it be: Life from the

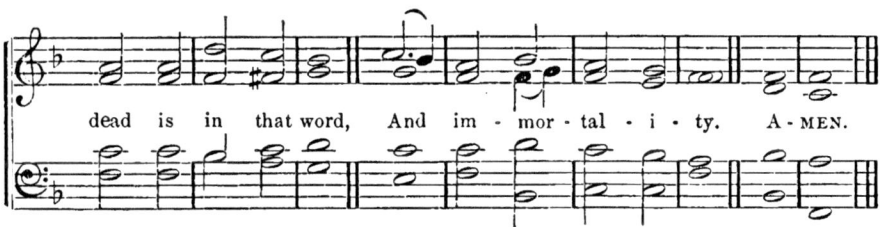

dead is in that word, And im - mor - tal - i - ty. A-MEN.

2 Here in the body pent,
  Absent from Him I roam,
Yet nightly pitch my moving tent
  A day's march nearer home.

3 My Father's house on high,
  Home of my soul, how near
At times to faith's foreseeing eye
  The golden gates appear!

4 My thirsty spirit faints
  To reach the land I love,
The bright inheritance of saints,
  Jerusalem above.

5 "For ever with the Lord!"
  Father, if 'tis Thy will,
The promise of that faithful word
  E'en here to me fulfill.

6 So, when my latest breath
  Shall rend the veil in twain,
By death I shall escape from death,
  And life eternal gain.

7 Knowing as I am known,
  How shall I love that word,
And oft repeat before the throne,
  "For ever with the Lord!" AMEN.

James Montgomery, 1835.

144 *There is a Land of Pure Delight.*

CANAAN. C. M.   Mrs. NORTON.

1. There is   a land of pure de-light Where saints im-mor - tal reign; In-

fin - ite day ex - cludes the night, And pleas - ures ban - ish   pain. There

ev - er - last - ing spring a - bides, And   nev - er - with-'ring flowers; Death,

like   a nar - row sea, di-vides This heav'nly land from ours. A - MEN.

2 Sweet fields, beyond the swelling flood,
   Stand dressed in living green :
So to the Jews old Canaan stood,
   While Jordan rolled between.
But tim'rous mortals start and shrink
   To cross this narrow sea,
And linger, shiv'ring, on the brink,
   And fear to launch away.

3 Oh, could we make our doubts remove,
   These gloomy doubts that rise,
And see the Canaan that we love
   With unbeclouded eyes,
Could we but climb where Moses stood,
   And view the landscape o'er,
Not Jordan's stream nor death's cold flood
   Should fright us from the shore. AMEN.

Dr. Watts.

145   *Jerusalem, Blest City.*

HESSE.   7s & 6s.   Arr. from HESSE.

1. Je - ru - sa - lem, blest cit - y, Name of ce - les - tial sound,

With liv-ing stones up - build - ed, With an - gel armies crowned, A - MEN.

2 Thou art the golden mansion
   Where saints for ever sing,
The seat of God's own chosen,
   The palace of our King.

3 There God for ever dwelleth,
   Himself of all the crown,

The Lamb a light there shineth.
   And never goeth down.

4 Naught to that city cometh
   Its people to molest;
They praise their God for ever,
   Nor day nor night they rest. AMEN.

146 *For thee, O dear, dear Country.*

BERNARD.   7s & 6s. D.

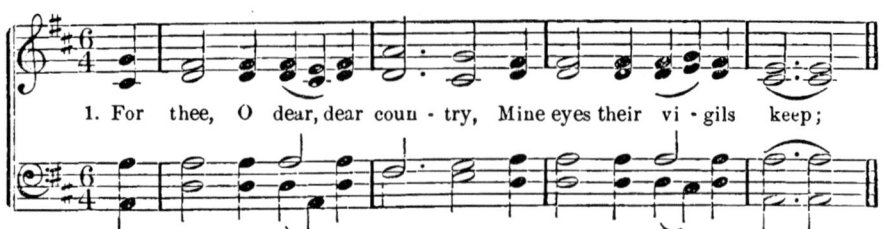

1. For   thee,   O dear, dear coun - try, Mine eyes their vi - gils   keep;

For ver - y   love be - hold - ing Thy hap - py name, they   weep.

D. C. ⊕

{ The men-tion of   thy glo - ry Is unc - tion to the breast, }   A - MEN.
{ And med - i - cine in sick-ness, And love and life and   rest. }

2 O one, O only mansion,
    O paradise of joy,
  Where tears are ever banished,
    And smiles have no alloy,
  The Lamb is all thy splendor,
    The Crucified thy praise,
  His laud and benediction
    Thy ransomed people raise.

3 With jasper glow thy bulwarks,
    Thy streets with emeralds blaze,
  The sardius and the topaz
    Unite in thee their rays;
  Thine ageless walls are bonded
    With amethyst unpriced,
  The saints build up its fabric,
    The Corner-stone is Christ.

4 Thou hast no shore, fair ocean,
  Thou hast no time, bright day,
Dear fountain of refreshment
  To pilgrims far away.
Upon the Rock of ages
  They raise thy holy tower;
Thine is the victor's laurel,
  And thine the golden dower.

5 O sweet and blessed country,
  The home of God's elect,
O sweet and blessed country,
  That eager hearts expect!
Jesu, in mercy bring us
  To that dear land of rest,
Who art, with God the Father,
  And Spirit, ever blest. AMEN.

H. Bernard. *Translated by Neale.*

147 *O God, our Help in Ages past.*

ST. ANN. C. M.   DENBY. (Arr. by Dr. CROFT.)

1. O God, our help in a-ges past, Our hope for years to come,
Our shel-ter from the stormy blast, And our e-ter-nal home. A-MEN.

2 Beneath the shadow of Thy throne
  Thy saints have dwelt secure;
Sufficient is Thine arm alone,
  And our defence is sure.

3 Before the hills in order stood
  Or earth received her frame,
From everlasting Thou art God,
  To endless years the same.

4 A thousand ages in Thy sight
  Are like an evening gone,

Short as the watch that ends the night
  Before the rising sun.

5 Time, like an ever-rolling stream,
  Bears all its sons away;
They fly forgotten, as a dream
  Dies at the opening day.

6 O God, our help in ages past,
  Our hope for years to come,
Be Thou our guard while troubles last,
  And our eternal home. AMEN.

Isaac Watts, 1719.

148   *No, no, it is not Dying.*

CECIL. 7s & 6s.   A. NEVIN.

1. No, no, it is not dy - ing,   No, no, it is not dy-ing,

To go un - to our God;   This gloom- y earth for - sak - ing,

Our jour - ney homeward tak - ing   A - long the star - ry road,

A - long the star - ry road.   A - - MEN.

2 ||: No, no, it is not dying, :||
   Heaven's citizen to be,
A crown immortal wearing,
And rest unbroken sharing,
   From care and conflict free.

3 ||: No, no, it is not dying, :||
   To hear this gracious word :
" Receive a Father's blessing,
For evermore possessing
   The favor of thy Lord."

4 ||: No, no, it is not dying, :||
   The Shepherd's voice to know ;

His sheep He ever leadeth,
His peaceful flock He feedeth,
   Where living pastures grow.

5 ||: No, no, it is not dying, :||
   To wear a lordly crown,
Among God's people dwelling,
The glorious triumph swelling
   Of Him whose sway we own

6 ||: Oh no, it is not dying, :||
   Thou Saviour of mankind ;
There streams of love are flowing,
No hindrance ever knowing ;
   Here drops alone we find. AMEN.

149   *It is not Death to Die.*

MOCCAS. S. M.   A. R. REINAGLE.

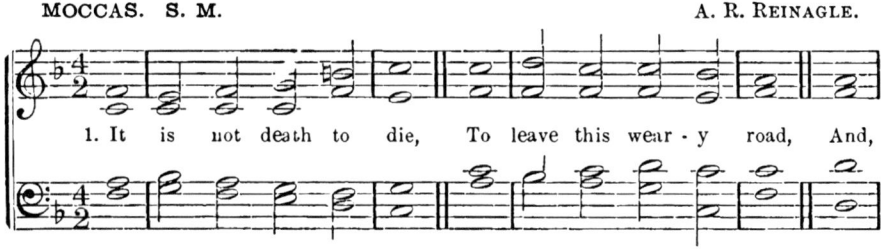

1. It is not death to die, To leave this wear - y road, And,

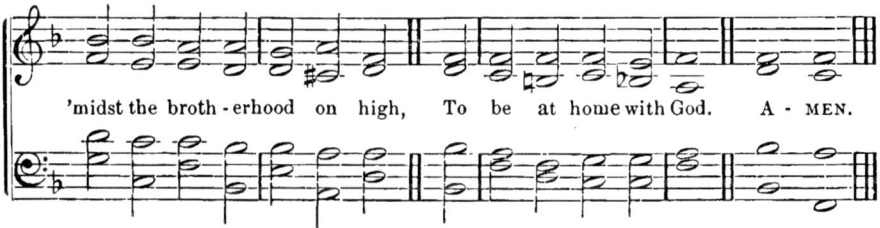

'midst the broth - erhood on high, To be at home with God. A - MEN.

2 It is not death to close
   The eye long dimmed by tears,
And wake, in glorious repose
   To spend eternal years.

3 It is not death to fling
   Aside this sinful dust,

And rise, on strong exulting wing,
   To live among the just.

4 Jesus, Thou Prince of life,
   Thy chosen cannot die :
Like Thee, they conquer in the strife,
   To reign with Thee on high. AMEN.

           George W. Bethune, 1847.

150　　*Tender Shepherd, Thou hast Still'd.*

MEINHOLD.　7s & 8s.　　　　　　　　　　　German. (BACH.)

1. Ten - der　Shep - herd, Thou　hast　still'd　Now　Thy　lit - tle
　　Ah,　how　peace - ful,　pale,　and　mild,　In　its　nar - row

lamb's　brief　weep - ing;　}
bed　'tis　sleep - ing,　}　And　no　sigh　of　an - guish　sore

Heaves　that　lit - tle　bo - som　more.　A - MEN.

2 In this world of care and pain,
　　Lord, Thou wouldst no longer leave
　　　it;
To the sunny heavenly plain
　　Thou dost now with joy receive it;
Clothed in robes of spotless white,
Now it dwells with Thee in light.

3 Ah, Lord Jesu, grant that we
　　Where it lives may soon be living,
And the lovely pastures see
　　That its heavenly food are giving;
Then the gain of death we prove, .
Though Thou take what most we love.
　　　　　　　　　　AMEN.
　　　　　　Tr. by Winckworth.

151   *When Morning Gilds the Skies.*

MORNING. 6s.   JOSEPH BARNBY, 1868.

1. When morning gilds the skies, My heart a - wak - ing cries,

May Je - sus Christ be praised. A - like at work and prayer,

To Je - sus I re - pair; May Je - sus Christ be praised. A - MEN.

2 Whene'er the sweet church-bell
Peals over hill and dell,
  May Jesus Christ be praised;
Oh, hark to what it sings,
As joyously it rings,
  May Jesus Christ be praised !

3 Does sadness fill my mind?
A solace here I find,
  May Jesus Christ be praised;
Or fades my earthly bliss?
My comfort still is this,
  May Jesus Christ be praised.

4 The night becomes as day
When from the heart we say,
  "May Jesus Christ be praised;"
The powers of darkness fear
When this sweet chant they hear,
  "May Jesus Christ be praised."

5 In heaven's eternal bliss
The loveliest strain is this,
  "Let Jesus Christ be praised;"
Let earth and sea and sky
From depth to height reply,
  "May Jesus Christ be praised."
                  AMEN.

152 *The Sands of Time are Sinking.*

MORNING STAR. 7s, 6s & 5.   Rev. Edward Seymour.

1. The sands of time are sink-ing, The dawn of hea-ven breaks,
The sum-mer morn I've sighed for, The fair sweet morn, a-wakes;
Dark, dark hath been the mid-night, But day-spring is at hand,
And glo-ry, glo-ry dwelleth In Em-man-uel's land. A-MEN.

2 O Christ! He is the fountain,
   The deep sweet well of love;
   The streams on earth I've tasted,
    More deep I'll drink above.
There to an ocean fullness
   His mercy doth expand,
And glory, glory dwelleth
   In Emmanuel's land.

3 With mercy and with judgment
   My web of time He wove,
And aye the dews of sorrow
   Were lustred with His love;

I'll bless the hand that guided,
   I'll bless the heart that planned,
When throned where glory dwelleth,
   In Emmanuel's land.

4 I've wrestled on toward heaven,
   'Gainst storm and wind and tide;
Now, like a weary traveler
   That leaneth on his guide,
Amid the shades of evening,
   While sinks life's lingering sand,
I hail the glory dawning
   From Emmanuel's land. AMEN.

153   As the Sun doth Daily Bise.

INNOCENTS. 7s.   THIBAUT.

1. As the sun doth dai - ly rise, Bright'ning all the morn - ing skies,

So to Thee with one ac - cord Lift we up our hearts, O Lord! A - MEN.

2 Day by day provide us food,
   For from Thee come all things good;
   Strength unto our souls afford
   From Thy living Bread, O Lord!

3 Be our Guard in sin and strife,
   Be the Leader of our life;
   Lest like sheep we stray abroad,
   Stay our wayward feet, O Lord.

4 Quickened by the Spirit's grace,
   All Thy holy will to trace,
   While we daily search Thy Word,
   Wisdom true impart, O Lord!

5 When the sun withdraws his light,
   When we seek our beds at night,
   Thou, by sleepless hosts adored,
   Hear the prayer of faith, O Lord.

6 When the hours are dark and drear,
   When the Tempter lurketh near,
   By Thy strength'ning grace outpoured,
   Save the tempted ones, O Lord.

7 Praise we with the heavenly host,
   Father, Son, and Holy Ghost;
   Thee would we with one accord
   Praise and magnify, O Lord. AMEN.
King Alfred, 900. Trans. by Earl Nelson, 1864.

154   *Awake, my Soul, and with the Sun.*

MORNING HYMN. L. M.   BARTHOLEMON.

1. A - wake, my soul, and with the sun Thy dai - ly

course of du - ty run; Shake off dull sloth, and ear - ly

rise To pay thy morn - ing sac - ri - fice. A - MEN.

2 Redeem thy misspent moments past,
  And live this day as if thy last;
  Thy talents to improve take care,
  For the great day thyself prepare

3 Let all thy converse be sincere,
  Thy conscience like the noonday clear,
  Think how all-seeing God thy ways
  And all thy secret thoughts surveys.

4 Awake, lift up thyself, my heart,
  And with the angels bear thy part,
  Who all night long unwearied sing,
  "High glory to th' eternal King."

5 All praise to Thee, who safe hast kept
  And hast refreshed me whilst I slept;

Grant, Lord, when I from death shall
  wake,
I may of endless life partake.

6 Lord, I my vows to Thee renew;
  Disperse my sins as morning dew,
  Guard my first springs of thought and
    will,
  And with Thyself my spirit fill.

7 Direct, control, suggest, this day
  All I design or do or say,
  That all my powers with all their might,
  In Thy sole glory may unite.   AMEN.

Thomas Ken, 1697.

155 *Abide with me : Fast falls the Eventide.*

EVENTIDE. 10s.

W. H. MONK.

1. A - bide with me: fast falls the e - ven - tide; The dark-ness deep-ens;

Lord, with me a - bide: When oth-er help-ers fail and comforts flee,

Help of the help-less, Oh a - bide with me. A - MEN.

2 Swift to its close ebbs out life's little day,
Earth's joys grow dim, its glories pass away,
Change and decay in all around I see;
O Thou who changest not, abide with me.

3 I need Thy presence every passing hour:
What but Thy grace can foil the tempter's power?
Who like Thyself my guide and stay can be?
Through cloud and sunshine, Lord, abide with me.

4 I fear no foe with Thee at hand to bless,
Ills have no weight, and tears no bitterness.
Where is death's sting? where, grave, thy victory?
I triumph still if Thou abide with me.

5 Hold Thou Thy cross before my closing eyes,
Shine through the gloom and point me to the skies;
Heaven's morning breaks, and earth's vain shadows flee;
In life, in death, O Lord, abide with me. AMEN.

Rev. H. F. Lyte.

156   *Sun of my Soul, Thou Saviour Dear.*

HURSLEY. L. M.   German. (W. H. MONK.)

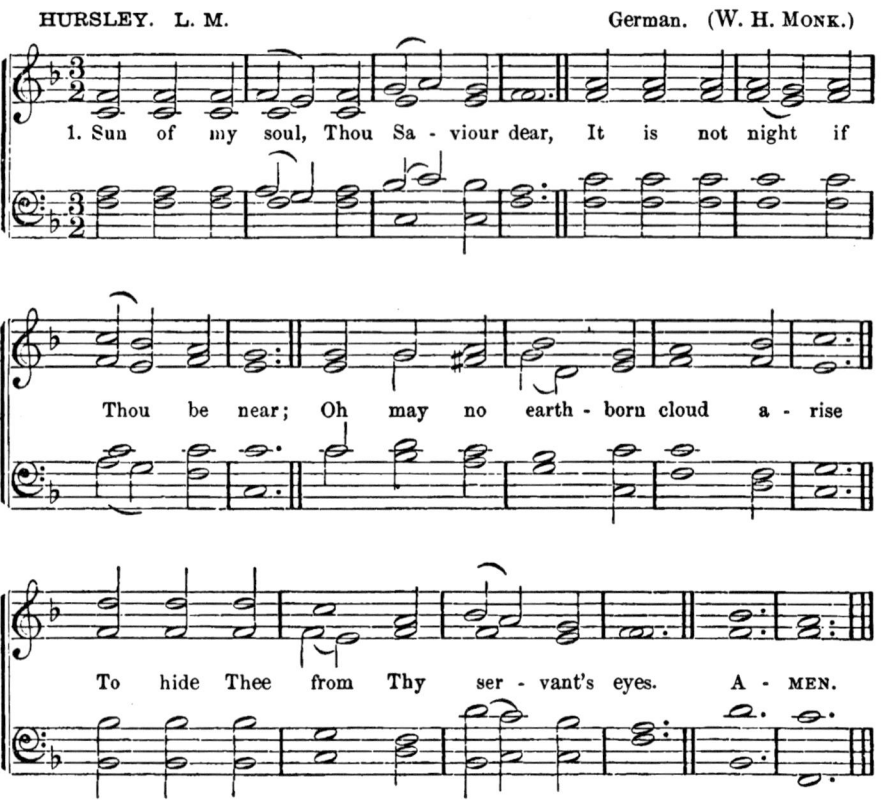

1. Sun of my soul, Thou Sa - viour dear, It is not night if Thou be near; Oh may no earth - born cloud a - rise To hide Thee from Thy ser - vant's eyes. A - MEN.

2 When the soft dews of kindly sleep
My wearied eyelids gently steep,
Be my last thought, "How sweet to rest
For ever on my Saviour's breast!"

3 Abide with me from morn till eve,
For without Thee I cannot live;
Abide with me when night is nigh,
For without Thee I dare not die.

4 If some poor wandering child of thine
Have spurned to-day the voice divine,

Now, Lord, the gracious work begin,
Let him no more lie down in sin.

5 Watch by the sick, enrich the poor
With blessings from Thy boundless
store;
Be every mourner's sleep to-night,
Like infant slumbers, pure and light.

6 Come near and bless us when we wake,
Ere through the world our way we take,
Till in the ocean of Thy love
We lose ourselves in heaven above.
AMEN.
Rev. J. Keble.

157 *Softly now the Light of Day.*

TWILIGHT. 7s. D.

G. A.

1. Soft-ly now the light of day Fades up - on my sight a - way;

Free from care, from la - bor free, Lord, I would commune with thee;
D.S. Par - don each in - firm - i - ty, O - pen fault, and se - cret sin.

Thou whose all-per - vading eye Naught escapes without, with - in, A - MEN.

2 Soon for me the light of day
Shall for ever pass away;
Then, from sin and sorrow free,
Take me, Lord, to dwell with Thee.

11

Thou who, sinless, yet hast known
All of man's infirmity,
Then from Thine eternal throne,
Jesus, look with pitying eye.

158   *Sweet Saviour, Bless us Ere we Go.*

COMPLINE.   8s.

ANON.

1. Sweet Sa - viour, bless us   ere   we   go,   Thy   word   in - to   our

minds   in - still,   And   make   our   luke - warm   hearts   to   glow   With

low - ly   love   and   fer - vent   will. Through life's   long   day   and

death's dark night,   O   gen - tle   Je - sus,   be   our   Light. A - MEN.

2 The day is gone, its hours have run,
  And Thou hast taken count of all—
The scanty triumphs grace hath won,
  The broken vow, the frequent fall.
Through life's long day and death's
    dark night,
  O gentle Jesus, be our Light.

3 Grant us, dear Lord, from evil ways
  True absolution and release,
And bless us, more than in past days,
  With purity and inward peace.

Through life's long day and death's
    dark night,
  O gentle Jesus, be our Light.

4 For all we love, the poor, the sad,
  The sinful, unto Thee we call;
Oh let Thy mercy make us glad,
  Thou art our Jesus and our All.
Through life's long day and death's
    dark night,
  O gentle Jesus, be our Light. AMEN.

Rev. F. W. Faber.

159   *Saviour, ere in Sweet Repose.*

WEBER. 7s.

C. M. VON WEBER.

1. Sa - viour, ere in sweet re - pose I my wear - y eye - lids close,

Let me love with per - fect love Child and man, and God a-bove. A-MEN.

2 Guard me when in sleep I lie,
  Plead for me with God on high;
All that stained my soul to-day,
  Wash it in Thy blood away.

3 If my slumbers broken be,
  Waking, let me think of Thee;
Darkness cannot make me fear
  If I feel that Thou art near. AMEN.

160 *The Day is Past and Over.*

ST. ANATOLIUS. P. M.   H. BROWN.

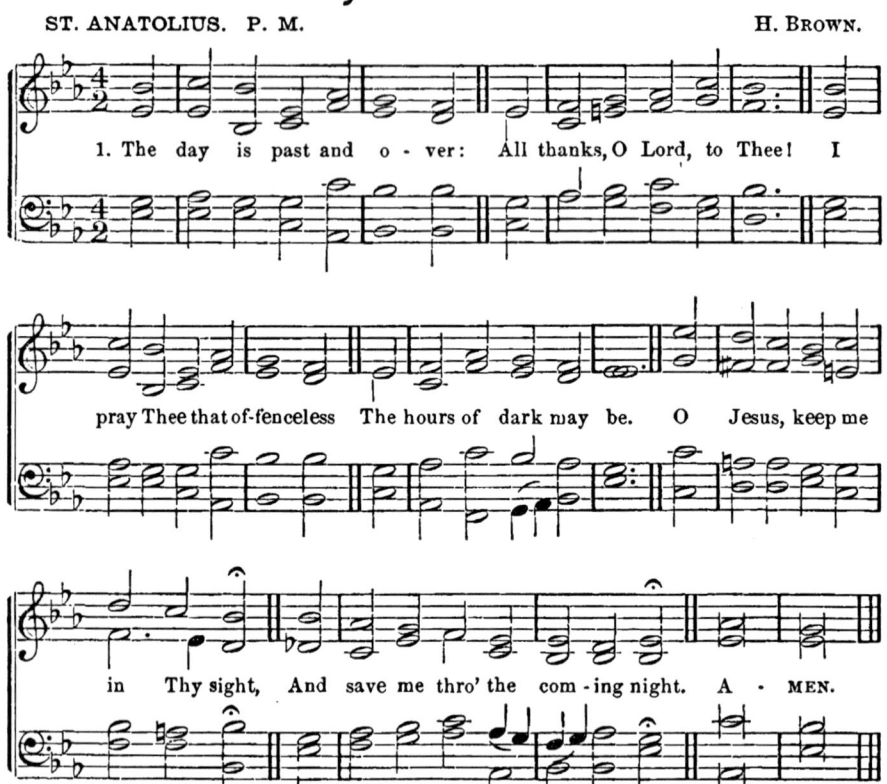

1. The day is past and o - ver: All thanks, O Lord, to Thee! I
pray Thee that of-fenceless The hours of dark may be. O Jesus, keep me
in Thy sight, And save me thro' the com - ing night. A - MEN.

2 The joys of day are over:
   I lift my heart to Thee,
And call on Thee that sinless
   The hours of gloom may be.
O Jesus, make their darkness light,
And save me through the coming night.

3 The toils of day are over:
   I raise the hymn to Thee,
And ask that free from peril
   The hours of fear may be.
O Jesus, keep me in Thy sight,
And guard me through the coming night.

4 Lighten mine eyes, O Saviour,
   Or sleep in death shall I,
And he, my wakeful tempter,
   Triumphantly shall cry,
"Against him I have now prevailed;
Rejoice! the child of God has failed."

5 Be Thou my soul's Preserver,
   O God, for Thou dost know
How many are the perils
   Through which I have to go.
O loving Jesus, hear my call,
And guard and save me from them all.
             AMEN.
            St. Anatolius.

161   *Glory to Thee, my God, this Night.*

TALLIS'S EVENING HYMN. **L. M.**   TALLIS.

1. Glo - ry to Thee, my God, this night, For all the bless - ings
of the light; Keep me, oh keep me, King of kings,
Un - der Thine own al - might - y wings. A - MEN.

2 Forgive me, Lord, for Thy dear Son,
  The ills that I this day have done,
  That with the world, myself, and Thee
  I, ere I sleep, at peace may be.

3 Teach me to live that I may dread
  The grave as little as my bed;
  Teach me to die that so I may
  Triumphing rise at the last day.

4 Oh may my soul on Thee repose,
  And with sweet sleep mine eyelids close,

Sleep that may me more vigorous make
To serve my God when I awake.

5 When in the night I sleepless lie,
  My soul with heavenly thoughts supply;
  Let no ill dreams disturb my rest,
  No powers of darkness me molest.

6 Oh when shall I, in endless day,
  For ever chase dark sleep away,
  And hymns divine with angels sing,
  Glory to Thee, eternal King? AMEN.
                              Tallis.

162   *The Church's one Foundation.*

AURELIA.   7s & 6s.   Dr. S. S. Wesley.

1. The Church's one Foun-da-tion Is Je-sus Christ, her Lord;

She is His new cre-a-tion By wa-ter and the Word:

From heav'n He came and sought her To be His ho-ly Bride;

With His own blood He bought her, And for her life He died. A-men.

2 Elect from every nation,
  Yet one o'er all the earth,
Her charter of salvation
  One Lord, one Faith, one Birth;
One holy name she blesses,
  ˑPartakes one holy Food,
And to one hope she presses,
  With every grace endued.

3 Though with a scornful wonder
  Men see her sore opprest,
By schisms rent asunder,
  By heresies distrest,

Yet saints their watch are keeping,
  Their cry goes up, " How long?"
And soon the night of weeping
  Shall be the morn of song.

4 'Mid toil and tribulation,
  And tumult of her war,
She waits the consummation
  Of peace for evermore,
Till with the vision glorious ˑ
  Her longing eyes are blest,
And the great Church victorious
  Shall be the Church at rest. AMEN.

163   *Oh Praise the Lord!*

NAGELI. 11s & 8.   NAGELI. (Arr. by W. B. HALL.)

1. Oh praise the Lord! He loves to hear you sing-ing; In sweet ac - cord loud let His praise be ringing. Oh praise the Lord, oh praise the Lord! A - MEN.

2 Our voices raise, with joy and gladness singing,
  And cheerful praise, oh let us all be bringing;
    Our voices raise, our voices raise.

3 We bless Thee, Lord, while every heart rejoices,
  Thy name adored we sing with reverent voices;
    We bless Thee, Lord, we bless Thee, Lord.

4 Then evermore, in every land and nation,
  Tell o'er and o'er the story of salvation,
    For evermore, for evermore. AMEN.

164   *Lead, kindly Light.*

LUX BENIGNA. P. M.   Dr. DYKES.

1. Lead, kindly Light a-mid th'encircling gloom,   Lead Thou me   on;

The night is dark, and I am far from   home;   Lead Thou   me   on.

Keep Thou my   feet;   I   do not ask   to   see . . . . .

The dis - tant   scene; one step e - nough   for   me.   A - MEN.

2 I was not ever thus, nor pray'd that Thou
　　Shouldst lead me on;
　I loved to choose and see my path, but
　　now
　　　Lead Thou me on.
　I loved the garish day, and, spite of fears,
　Pride ruled my will; remember not
　　past years.

3 So long Thy power hast blest me, sure
　　it still
　　Will lead me on　　　　[rent, till
　O'er moor and fen, o'er crag and tor-
　　The night is gone,　　　[smile,
　And with the morn those angel-faces
　Which I have loved long since, and
　　lost a while. AMEN.

Dr. J. H. Newman.

165　　*Lord, Dismiss us with Thy Blessing.*

SICILIAN HYMN.　8s & 7s.　　　　　　　　　　ITALIAN.

1. Lord, dis - miss us with Thy bless-ing, Fill our hearts with joy and peace; { Let us each, Thy love pos - sess - ing, / Oh re - fresh us, Oh re - fresh us, } Tri - umph in re - deem - ing grace. } Trav - 'ling through this wil - der - ness. } A - MEN.

2 Thanks we give, and adoration,
　For Thy gospel's joyful sound;
　May the fruits of Thy salvation
　In our hearts and lives abound;
　　May Thy presence
　With us evermore be found.

3 So, whene'er the signal's given,
　Us from earth to call away,
　Borne on angels' wings to heaven,
　Glad the summons to obey,
　　We shall surely
　Reign with Christ in endless day.

AMEN.　*Rev. W. Shirley*

166   *Drightly Gleams our Banner.*

ST. ALBANS.   6s & 5s.   From HAYDN.   (Arr. by Rev. J. B. DYKES.)

1. Bright-ly gleams our ban - ner,   Point - ing to the sky,
CHO.—Bright-ly gleams our ban - ner,   Point - ing to the sky,

Wav - ing wand'rers on - ward   To their home on high.
Wav - ing wand'rers on - ward   To their home on high.

Journeying o'er a des - ert,   Glad - ly thus we pray,

And, with hearts u - ni - ted, Take our heav'nward way.   A - MEN.

2 Hail, sweet Jesus, Master!
　　Round Thy sacred feet,
　Here, with hearts rejoicing,
　　See Thy children meet.
　Long, alas! we've left Thee,
　　Straying far away;
　Now once more we'll enter
　　On the narrow way.
Cho.—Brightly gleams our banner, etc.

3 All our days direct us,
　　Make us meek and mild
　By Thy childhood's pattern,
　　Mary's holy Child.

Bid Thine angels shield us
　　When the storm-clouds lower;
　Pardon Thou, protect us
　　At death's solemn hour.—*Cho.*

4 Jesu, saints and angels
　　With Thy Church combine,
　Offering prayers and praises
　　At Thy glorious shrine;
　When the toil is over,
　　Then comes rest and peace,
　Jesus in His beauty,
　　Songs that never cease.—*Cho.*
　　　　　　　　　　AMEN.

167　*God shall Charge His Angel Legions.*

TRUST.　8s & 7s.　　　　　　　　　　MENDELSSOHN.

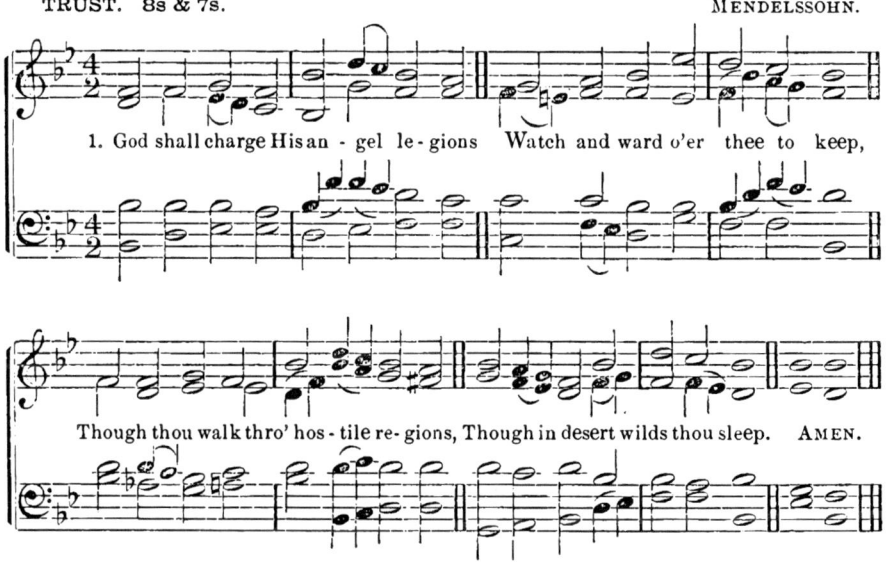

1. God shall charge His an - gel le - gions Watch and ward o'er thee to keep,

Though thou walk thro' hos - tile re - gions, Though in desert wilds thou sleep.　AMEN.

2 On the lion vainly roaring,
　　On his young, thy foot shall tread,
　And, the dragon's den exploring,
　　Thou shalt bruise the serpent's head.

3 Since, with pure and firm affection,
　　Thou on God hast set thy love,

With the wings of His protection
　　He will shield thee from above.

4 Thou shalt call on Him in trouble,
　　He will hearken, He will save,
　Here for grief reward thee double,
　　Crown with life beyond the grave.
　　　　　　　　　　AMEN.
　　　　　　　　J. Montgomery.

168   *Oft in Sorrow.*

CONFIDENCE.   7s.   SIR JOHN GOSS.

1. Oft in sor - row, oft in woe, On - ward, Christians, on - ward go;

Fight the fight, maintain the strife, Strengthened with the Bread of life.

Let your droop - ing hearts be glad, March with heav'n-ly ar - mor clad;

Fight, nor think the bat - tle long; Vic - t'ry soon shall turn your song. A - MEN.

2 Let not sorrow dim your eye,
  Soon shall every tear be dry ;
  Let not woe your course impede,
  Great your strength if great your need ;

Onward, then, to battle move,
More than conquerors ye shall prove ;
Though opposed by many a foe,
Christian soldiers, onward go.   AMEN.
Henry Kirke White.

169   *From Greenland's Icy Mountains.*

MISSIONARY HYMN.   7s & 6s. D.   LOWELL MASON.

1. From Greenland's icy mountains, From India's coral strand, Where Afric's sunny fountains

Roll down their golden sand, From many an ancient river, From many a palmy plain,

They call us to de - liv - er Their land from error's chain.   A - MEN.

2 What though the spicy breezes
  Blow soft o'er Ceylon's isle,
Though every prospect pleases,
  And only man is vile?
In vain with lavish kindness
  The gifts of God are strown,
The heathen, in his blindness,
  Bows down to wood and stone.

3 Shall we whose souls are lighted
  With wisdom from on high,
Shall we to men benighted
  The lamp of life deny?

Salvation! oh, salvation!
  The joyful sound proclaim,
Till earth's remotest nation
  Has learned Messiah's name.

4 Waft, waft, ye winds, his story,
  And you, ye waters, roll,
Till, like a sea of glory,
  It spreads from pole to pole,
Till o'er our ransomed nature
  The Lamb for sinners slain,
Redeemer, King, Creator,
  In bliss returns to reign.   AMEN.
                 Bishop Heber.

170 Onward, Christian Soldiers.

ST. GERTRUDE. 6s & 5s. ARTHUR SULLIVAN.

1. Onward, Christian sol - diers, Marching as to war, With the cross of Je - sus

Go-ing on be - fore. Christ, the roy-al Mas - ter, Leads a-gainst the foe;

Forward in - to bat - tle See His banners go. *CHORUS.* Onward, Christian sol - diers,

Marching as to war, With the cross of Je - sus Go-ing on be - fore. A - MEN.

2 At the sign of triumph
　Satan's host doth flee;
On, then, Christian soldiers,
　On to victory.
Hell's foundations quiver
　At the shout of praise;
Brothers, lift your voices,
　Loud your anthems raise.—*Cho.*

3 Crowns and thrones may perish,
　Kingdoms rise and wane,
But the Church of Jesus
　Constant will remain;

Gates of hell can never
　'Gainst that Church prevail,
We have Christ's own promise,
　And that cannot fail.—*Cho.*

4 Onward, then, ye people,
　Join our happy throng;
Blend with ours your voices
　In the triumph-song;
Glory, laud, and honor
　Unto Christ the King—
This, through countless ages,
　Men and angels sing.—*Cho.*
　　　　　　　AMEN.

171　*God Bless our Native Land.*

AMERICA.　6s & 4s.　　　　　　　　　　　　H. CAREY.

1. God bless our native land! Firm may she ever stand　　When the wild tempests rave,
Thro' storm and night;

Ruler of winds and wave, Do Thou our country save By Thy great might.　A - MEN.

2 For her our prayer shall rise
　To God above the skies,
　　On Him we wait;
Thou who art ever nigh,
Guardian with watchful eye,
To Thee alone we cry,
　"God save the State."

3 Our fathers' God, to Thee,
　Author of liberty,
　　To Thee we sing;
Long may our land be bright
With freedom's holy light;
Protect us by Thy might,
　Great God, our King. AMEN.
　　　　　　J. S. Dwight.

172   *O Happy Band of Pilgrims.*

PILGRIM.   7s & 6s.   HAUPTMANN.

1. O hap-py band of pilgrims, If on-ward ye will tread,

With Je - sus as your Fel - low, To Je - sus as your

Head,   To Je - sus as your Head,—   A - MEN.

2 Oh happy if ye labor
  As Jesus did for men,
Oh happy if ye hunger
  As Jesus hungered then.

3 The cross that Jesus carried
  He carried as your due,
The crown that Jesus weareth,
  He weareth it for you.

4 The faith by which ye see Him,
  The hope in which ye yearn,
The love that through all troubles
  To Him alone will turn,

5 The trials that beset you,
  The sorrows ye endure,
The manifold temptations
  That death alone can cure,—

6 What are they but His jewels
  Of right celestial worth?
What are they but the ladder
  Set up to heaven on earth?

7 O happy band of pilgrims,
  Look upward to the skies,
Where such a light affliction
  Shall win so great a prize. AMEN.

173   *Waken, Christian Children.*

English.

1. Waken, Christian chil - dren, Up, and let us sing, With glad hearts and voi- ces,

Of our new-born King. Up! 'tis meet to wel - come With a joyous lay

Christ, the King of glo - ry, Born for us to - day. A - MEN.

2 In a manger lowly
  Sleeps the heavenly Child,
O'er Him fondly bendeth
  Mary, mother mild.
Far above that stable,
  Up in heaven so high,
One bright star outshineth,
  Watching silently.

3 Fear not, then, to enter,
  Though we cannot bring
Gold or myrrh or incense
  Fitting for a King.
  12

Gifts He asketh richer,
  Offering costlier still,
Yet may Christian children
  Bring them if they will.

4 Brighter than all jewels
  Shines the modest eye;
Best of gifts, He loveth
  Infant purity.
Haste we, then, to welcome
  With a joyous lay
Christ, the King of glory,
  Born for us to-day.

174   *Holy Night ! Peaceful Night.*

Michael Haydn.

1. Ho - ly night!   peace-ful night!   All   is   dark,   save the light

Yon - der where they sweet vig - il keep   O'er   the   Babe who in   si - lent sleep

Rests   in   hea - ven - ly   , peace,   Rests   in   hea - ven - ly   peace.

2 Holy night! peaceful night!
  Only for shepherds' sight
  Came blest visions of angel-throngs
  With their loud alleluia songs,
    Saying, Jesus is come,
    Saying, Jesus is come.

3 Holy night! peaceful night!
  Child of heaven, oh how bright [born !
  Thou didst smile on us when Thou wast
  Blest indeed was that happy morn,
    Full of heavenly joy,
    Full of heavenly joy.

175 *While Shepherds watched their Flocks by Night.*

From *The Shawm.*

1. While shepherds watch'd their flocks by night, All seat - ed on the ground,
The an - gel of the Lord came down, And glo - ry shone a - round.

Sing glo - ry, glo - ry, glo - ry, glo - ry, glo - ry,

glo - ry, glo - ry, glo - ry, glo - ry, glo - ry.

2 " Fear not," said he, for mighty dread
   Had seized their troubled mind ;
   " Glad tidings of great joy I bring
   To you and all mankind.

3 " To you, in David's town this day,
   Is born, of David's line,
   A Saviour, who is Christ the Lord,
   And this shall be the sign:

4 " The heavenly Babe you there shall
   find
   To human view displayed,

All meanly wrapt in swathing-bands,
   And in a manger laid."

5 Thus spake the seraph, and forthwith
   Appeared a shining throng
   Of angels praising God, who thus
   Addressed their joyful song

6 " All glory be to God on high,
   And to the earth be peace ;
   Good-will henceforth, from heaven to
   men,
   Begin, and never cease."

176   *Christ was Born on Christmas Day.*

A. NEVIN.

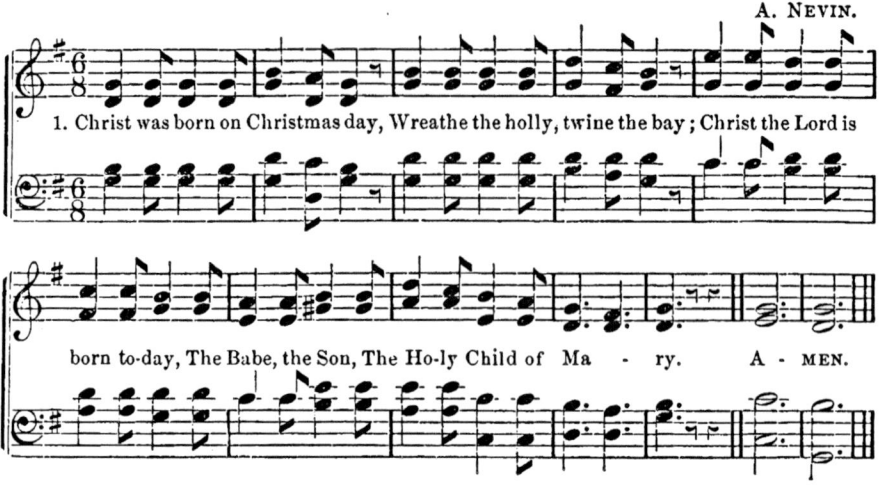

1. Christ was born on Christmas day, Wreathe the holly, twine the bay; Christ the Lord is born to-day, The Babe, the Son, The Ho-ly Child of Ma - ry.   A - MEN.

2 He is born to set us free,
  He is born our Lord to be,
  Carol, carol joyfully:
    The Babe, the Son, etc.

3 Let the bright red berries glow
  Everywhere in goodly show;
  Christ the Lord is come, you know,
    The Babe, the Son, etc.

4 Christian men, rejoice and sing;
  'Tis the birthday of our King;
  Every one your anthem bring
    To God the Lord,
    The holy Child of Mary.

177   *A Child this Day is Born.*

TRADITIONAL.

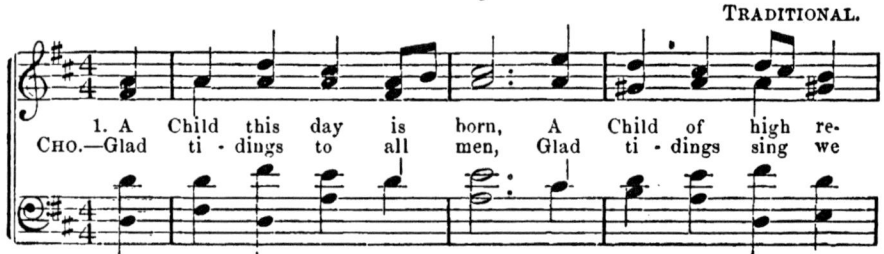

1. A Child this day is born, A Child of high re-
CHO.—Glad ti - dings to all men, Glad ti - dings sing we

A CHILD THIS DAY IS BORN.—Continued.

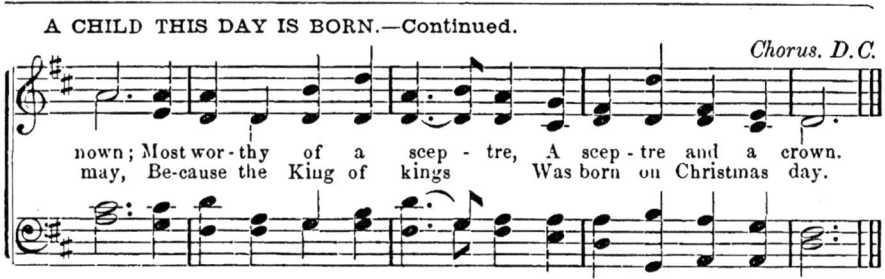

nown; Most wor-thy of a scep - tre, A scep - tre and a crown.
may, Be-cause the King of kings Was born on Christmas day.

2 These tidings shepherds heard
  Whilst watching o'er their fold;
'Twas by an angel unto them
  That night revealed and told.—*Cho.*

3 They praised the Lord our God,
  And our celestial King;

All glory be in Paradise,
  This heavenly host do sing.—*Cho.*

4 All glory be to God,
  That sitteth still on high,
With praises and with triumph great,
  And joyful melody.—*Cho.*

178 *The Children's King.*

ANON.

1. Now we bring our Christmas treasures, Loving tho'ts and deeds we bring;

Child-like hearts we glad-ly of - fer To the Child, the children's King. A - MEN.

2 To the Child who in the manger
  Lay upon that Christmas morn,
When the angels came to tell us
  That the children's King was born.

3 And He lives throughout the ages—
  Lives and reigns in earth and sky;

Angel hosts still sing the glory
  Of the children's King on high.

4 Yet He cares for children's praises,
  So with heart and voice we sing,
" Glory in the highest, glory
  To the Child, the children's King."
  AMEN.

179   *Little Children, can you Tell?*

1. Lit - tle chil - dren, can you tell,   Do you know the

sto - ry well,   Ev - 'ry girl and ev - 'ry boy,   Why the an - gels

sing   for joy   On   the   Christ-mas   morn - ing?

2 Yes, we know the story well;
Listen now and hear us tell,
Every girl and every boy,
Why the angels sing for joy
On the Christmas morning.

3 Shepherds sat upon the ground,
Fleecy flocks were scattered round,
When a brightness filled the sky,
And a voice was heard on high
On the Christmas morning.

4 "Joy and peace!" the angels sang;
Far the pleasant echoes rang;

"Peace on earth, to men good-will!"
Hark! the angels sing it still
On the Christmas morning.

5 For a little Babe that day
Cradled in a manger lay,
Born on earth our Lord to be;
This the wondering angels see
On the Christmas morning.

6 Joy our little hearts shall fill,
Peace and love, and all good-will;
This fair Babe of Bethlehem
Children loves, and blesses them
On the Christmas morning.

180   *The Easter Morning.*

L. H. REDNER.

1. Birds their ma - tin - car - ol sing, Dew-drops to the lil - ies cling,
On the East - er morn - ing, On the East - er morn - ing; When the an - gel
rob'd in white, Com - ing from the realms of light At the day's first dawn - ing,

2 Rolls the heavy stone away
  From the tomb where Jesus lay,
    Over Death victorious;
  Forth in radiant majesty
  From the grave's captivity
    Comes the Saviour glorious.

3 When the sun expels the night
  From the plain, and mountain-height
    Tips with rosy gleaming,

Then the Sun of righteousness
O'er the world's unhappiness
  Sheds His joyous beaming.

4 So into your hearts of sin,
  Children, let Him enter in
    At your life's first morning,
  That with beams of light divine
  He through all your lives may shine
    Till the heavenly dawning.

Rev. W. H. Neilson.

181   *We will Carol Joyfully.*

Arr. from KULLAR.

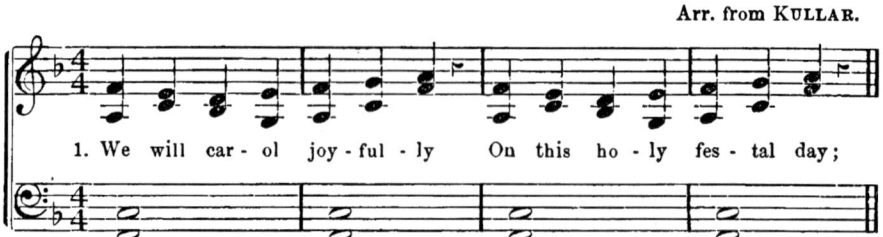

1. We will car - ol joy - ful - ly On this ho - ly fes - tal day;

To our ris - en Lord and King Grate-ful homage we will bring.

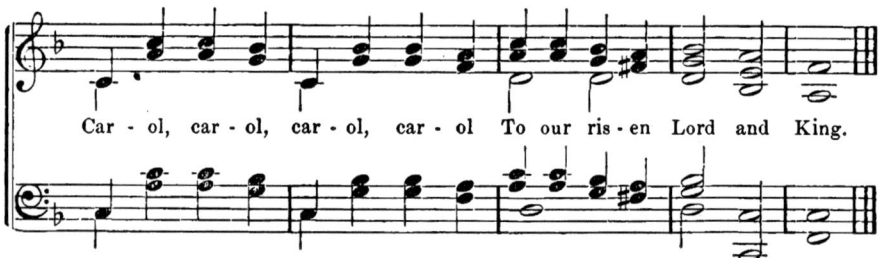

Car - ol, car - ol, car - ol, car - ol To our ris - en Lord and King.

2 We will carol joyfully
   As with sweet accord we bring
Praise from every heart and voice
To our risen Lord and King.
       Carol, carol, etc.

3 We will carol joyfully
   While our love and thanks we give

To our risen Lord and King,
   Him who died that we might live.
       Carol, carol, etc.

4 We will carol joyfully,
   And to Him our offerings bring—
Grateful hearts, with love and praise,
To our risen Lord and King.
       Carol, carol, etc.

182   *Smile Praises, O Sky!*

1. Smile prais - es, O sky! Soft breathe them, O air! Be - low and on

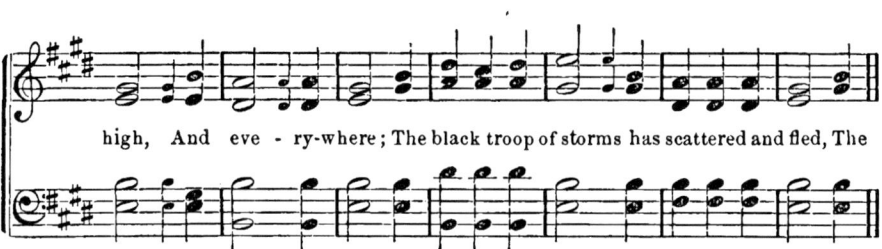

high, And eve - ry-where; The black troop of storms has scattered and fled, The

{ Lord hath a - ri - sen, The }
{ Lord hath a - ri - sen, un- } harmed from the dead.

2 Sweep tides of rich music
  The new world along,
And pour in full measure,
  Sweet lyres, your song.
Sing, sing, for He liveth,
  He lives, as He said;
The Lord has arisen
  Unharmed from the dead.

3 Clap, clap your hands, mountains;
  Ye valleys, resound;
Leap, leap for joy, fountains;
  Ye hills, catch the sound.
All triumph! He liveth,
  He lives, as He said;
The Lord has arisen
  Unharmed from the dead.

Tr. by Mrs. Charles.

11

183   *Christ hath Arisen.*

M. WERNER.

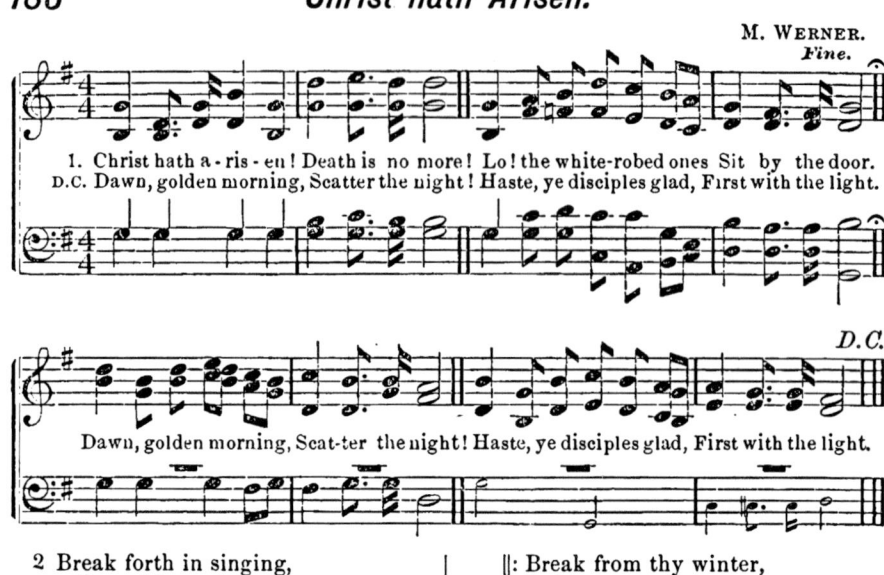

1. Christ hath a - ris - en! Death is no more! Lo! the white-robed ones Sit by the door.
D.C. Dawn, golden morning, Scatter the night! Haste, ye disciples glad, First with the light.

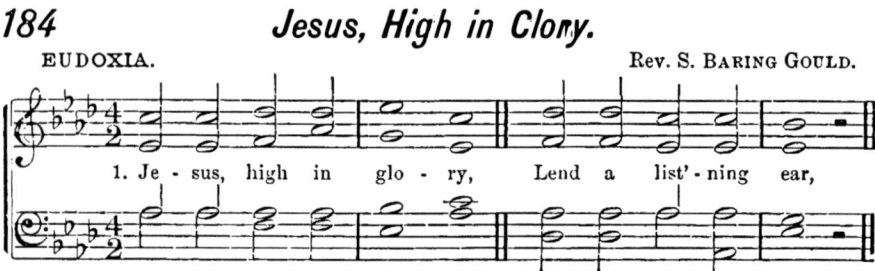

Dawn, golden morning, Scat-ter the night! Haste, ye disciples glad, First with the light.

2 Break forth in singing,
   O world new-born!
Chant the great Easter-tide,
   Christ's holy morn.
‖: Chant Him, young sunbeams,
   Dancing in mirth,
Chant, all ye winds of God,
   Coursing the earth. :‖

3 Chant Him, ye laughing flowers
   Fresh from the sod;
Chant Him, wild leaping streams,
   Praising your God.

‖: Break from thy winter,
   Sad heart, and sing;
Bud with thy blossoms fair,
   Christ is thy Spring. :‖

4 Come where the Lord hath lain;
   Past is the gloom;
See the full eye of day
   Smile through the tomb.
‖: Hark! angel-voices
   Fall from the skies
"Christ hath arisen!"
   Glad heart, arise. :‖

Rev. E. A. Washburn.

184   *Jesus, High in Glory.*

EUDOXIA.

Rev. S. BARING GOULD.

1. Je - sus, high in glo - ry, Lend a list' - ning ear,

EUDOXIA.—Continued.

When we bow be - fore Thee; Children's prais - es hear. A - MEN.

2 Though Thou art so holy,
  Heaven's almighty King,
Thou wilt stoop to listen
  When Thy praise we sing.

3 We are little children,
  Weak and apt to stray,
Saviour, guide and keep us
  In the heavenly way.

4 Save us, Lord, from sinning,
  Watch us day by day,
Help us now to love Thee,
  Take our sins away.

5 Then, when Jesus calls us
  To our heavenly home,
We would gladly answer,
  "Saviour, Lord, we come." AMEN.

185   *Humble Praises, Holy Jesus.*

RUSSIAN HYMN.

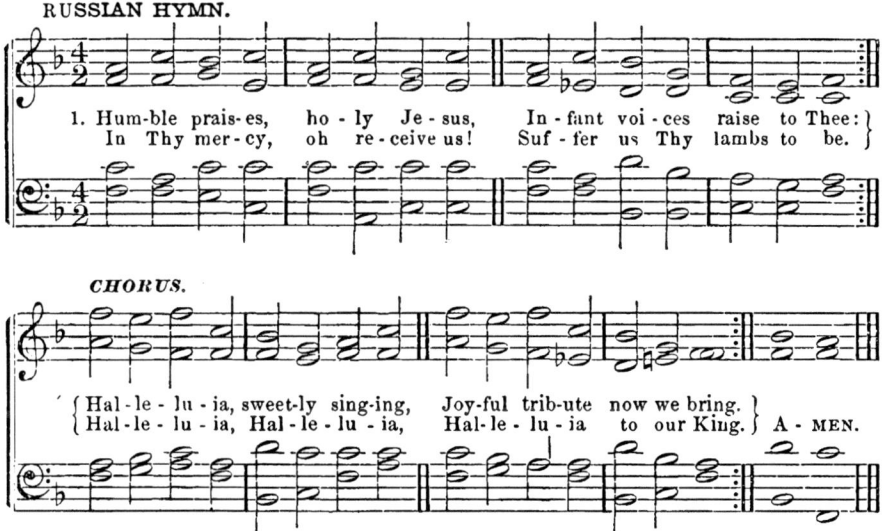

1. Hum-ble prais- es, ho - ly Je - sus, In - fant voi - ces raise to Thee:
In Thy mer - cy, oh re - ceive us! Suf - fer us Thy lambs to be.

CHORUS.

{ Hal - le - lu - ia, sweet-ly sing-ing, Joy-ful trib-ute now we bring. }
{ Hal - le - lu - ia, Hal - le - lu - ia, Hal - le - lu - ia to our King. } A - MEN.

2 Gracious Saviour, be Thou with us,
  Let Thy mercy richly flow;
Give Thy Spirit, blessed Jesus,
  Light and life on us bestow.
Cho.—Halleluia, sweetly singing, etc.

186   ## *O Lord, we Adore Thee.*

PANSERON.

1. O Lord, we a - dore Thee, Humbly we im - plore Thee, Keep us in Thy
care, Hear, oh hear our prayer. 1. And, Thou gracious Saviour, Oh, grant us Thy
2. As Thou hast, etc.
fa - vor; By Thy mortal suff'ring, Deign to bless our off'ring. A - MEN.

2 As Thou hast descended
And mortals befriended,
Still smile Thou upon us,
Look with mercy on us.
            O Lord, etc.

3 The angels do bless Thee;
Men too shall confess Thee,
Till Thy true salvation
Glad earth's every nation.
            O Lord, etc.

187   *Hosanna we Sing, like the Children Dear.*

HOSANNA.   E. A.

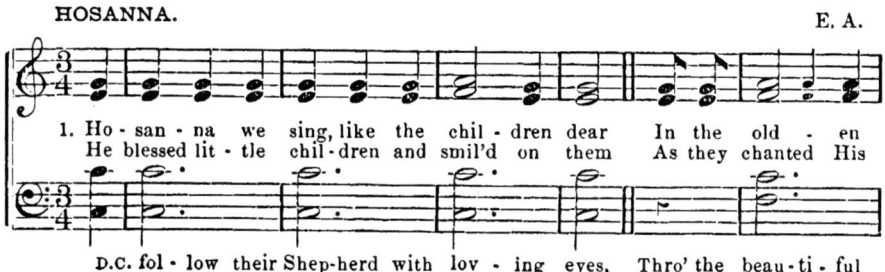

1. Ho - san - na we sing, like the chil - dren dear   In the old - en
He blessed lit - tle chil - dren and smil'd on them   As they chanted His

D.C. fol - low their Shep-herd with lov - ing eyes, Thro' the beau - ti - ful

days when the Lord liv'd here; }
praise in Je - ru - sa - lem. } Al - le - lu - ia! we sing like the child-ren bright;

val - leys of par - a - dise.

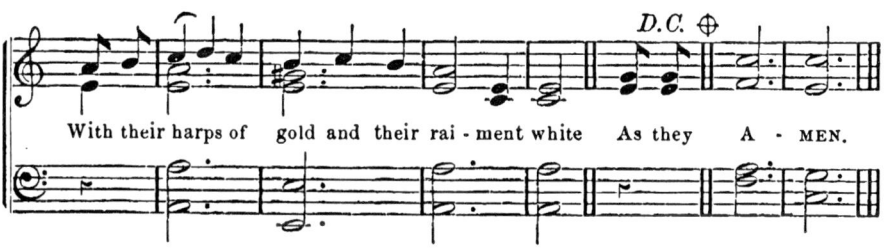

With their harps of gold and their rai - ment white   As they   A - MEN.

2 Hosanna we sing, for He lends His ear
And rejoices the hymns of His own to hear;
We know that His heart will never wax cold
To the lambs that He feeds in His earthly fold.
"Alleluia!" we sing in the Church we love,
"Alleluia!" resounds in the Church above;
To Thy little ones, Lord, may such grace be given
That we lose not our part in the song of heaven. AMEN.

188   *Praise, oh Praise our God and King!*

MONKLAND.   J. B. WILKES.

SEMI-CHORUS.

1. Praise, oh praise our God and King! Hymns of ad - o - ra - tion sing:

CHORUS.

For His mer-cies still en-dure, Ev - er faith-ful, ev - er sure. A - MEN.

2 Praise Him that He made the sun,
Day by day his course to run ;
For His mercies still endure,
Ever faithful, ever sure.

3 And the silver moon by night,
Shining with her gentle light;
For His mercies still endure,
Ever faithful, ever sure.

4 Praise Him that He gave the rain
To mature the swelling grain ;

For His mercies still endure,
Ever faithful, ever sure.

5 And hath bid the fruitful field
Crops of precious increase yield ;
For His mercies still endure,
Ever faithful, ever sure.

6 Glory to our bounteous King,
Glory let creation sing—
Glory to the Father, Son,
And blest Spirit, Three in One.
                                    AMEN.

189   *Jesus, Saviour, Son of God.*

ELSIE.   A. NEVIN.

1. Je - sus, Sa - viour, Son   of   God, Who   for   me   life's   path - way   trod,

ELSIE.—Continued.

Who for me be-came a child, Make me humble, meek, and mild. A - MEN.

2 I Thy little lamb would be,
Jesus, I would follow Thee;
Samuel was Thy child of old,
Take me, too, within Thy fold.

3 Teach me how to pray to Thee,
Make me holy, heavenly;
Let me love what Thou dost love,
Let me live with Thee above. AMEN.

190   *The Infant Martyrs.*

NETTLETON.   ANON.

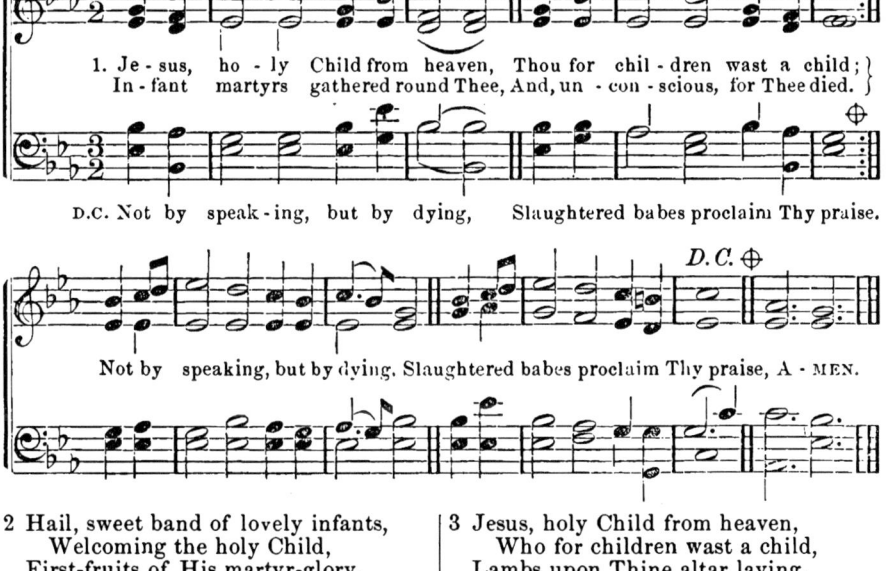

1. Je - sus, ho - ly Child from heaven, Thou for chil - dren wast a child;
In - fant martyrs gathered round Thee, And, un - con - scious, for Thee died.

D.C. Not by speak - ing, but by dying, Slaughtered babes proclaim Thy praise.

Not by speaking, but by dying, Slaughtered babes proclaim Thy praise, A - MEN.

2 Hail, sweet band of lovely infants,
Welcoming the holy Child,
First-fruits of His martyr-glory,
Innocent and meek and mild.
‖: Not by willing, but by dying,
They gave up their all for Thee. :‖

3 Jesus, holy Child from heaven,
Who for children wast a child,
Lambs upon Thine altar laying,
Make us humble, meek, and mild,
‖: That in living and in dying
We may evermore be Thine. AMEN.

191   *Little Travelers Zionward.*

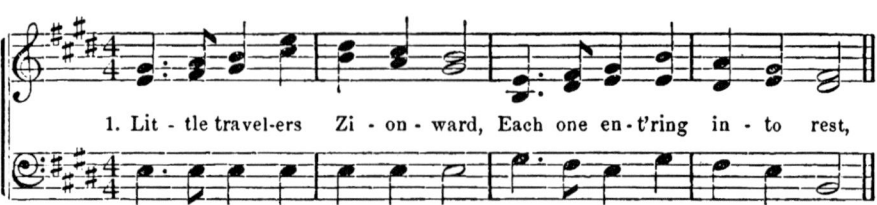

1. Lit - tle travel-ers Zi - on - ward, Each one en - t'ring in - to rest,

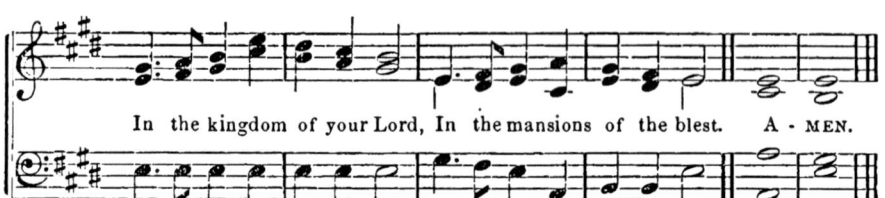

In the kingdom of your Lord, In the mansions of the blest. A - MEN.

2 There to welcome Jesus waits,
  Gives the crown His followers win;
Lift your heads, ye golden gates,
  Let the little travelers in.

3 Who are these whose little feet,
  Pacing life's dark journey through,
Soon shall reach that heavenly seat
  They had ever kept in view?

4 "I, from Greenland's frozen land;"
  "I, from India's sultry plain;"

"I, from Afrie's burning sand;"
"I, from islands of the main."

5 "All our earthly journey past,
  Every tear and pain gone by,
We'll together meet at last
  'At the portal of the sky."

6 Each the welcome "Come!" awaits,
  Conquerors over death and sin.
Lift your heads, ye golden gates,
  Let the little travelers in. AMEN.

192   *Holy Jesus, be my Light.*

MAUD.   A. S. GATTY.

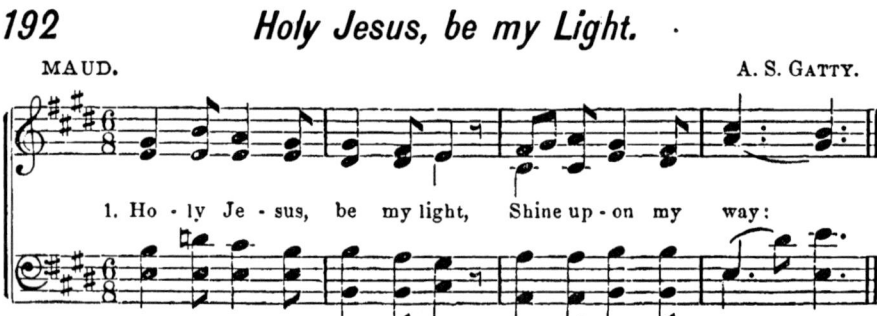

1. Ho - ly Je - sus, be my light, Shine up - on my way:

MAUD—Continued.

Through this tempting, changing life   Lead me day by   day.   A - MEN.

2 As the wise men came of old,
   Traveling afar,
Guided to Thy cradle throne
   By a wondrous star, ·

2 So be Thou my constant Guide,
   Lead me all the way,
Till I reach Thy home at last,
   Nevermore to stray.   AMEN.

193   *I am Jesus' Little Lamb.*

1. I am Je - sus' lit - tle lamb,   There-fore glad and gay I am;
D.C. Tends me ev' - ry day the same,   E - ven calls me by my name.

D.C.

Je- sus loves me, Je - sus knows me, All that's good and fair He shows me; A - MEN.

2 Out and in I safely go,
   Want and hunger never know;
Soft green pastures He discloseth,
Where His happy flock reposeth;
When I faint or thirsty be,
To the brook He leadeth me.
13

3 Should not I be glad and gay,
   In this blessed fold all day,
By this holy Shepherd tended,
Whose kind arms, when life is ended,
Bear me to the world of light
Yes, oh yes, my lot is bright. AMEN.

194   *Little Children, come to Jesus.*

S. B. SAXTON.   From *Musical Pioneer.*

1. Lit - tle chil - dren, come to Je - sus; Hear Him say - ing, "Come to me;"

Bless - ed Je - sus, who to save us Shed His blood on Cal - va - ry.

Lit - tle souls were made to serve Him, All His ho - ly law ful - fill;

Lit - tle hearts were made to love Him, Lit - tle hands to do His will. A - MEN.

2 Little eyes to read the Bible
  Given from the heavens above;
Little ears to hear the story
  Of the Saviour's wondrous love;

Little tongues to sing His praises,
  Little feet to walk His ways,
Little bodies to be temples
  Where the Holy Spirit stays. AMEN.

195   *The Fields are all White.*

Rev. W. H. COOKE.

1. The fields are all white, And the reap - ers are few; We chil - dren are will - ing, But what can we do To work for our Lord in His har - vest, To work for our Lord in His har - vest? A - MEN.

2 Our hands are so small,
   And our words are so weak,
   We cannot teach others;
   How, then, shall we seek
   To work for our Lord in His harvest?

3 We'll work by our prayers,
   By the pennies we bring,

By small self-denials;
   The least little thing
May work for our Lord in His harvest.

4 Until, by and by,
   As the years pass, at length
   We too may be reapers,
   And go forth in strength
To work for our Lord in His harvest.
   AMEN.

196   Where is the Holy Jesus ?

Rev. Dr. J. B. DYKES.

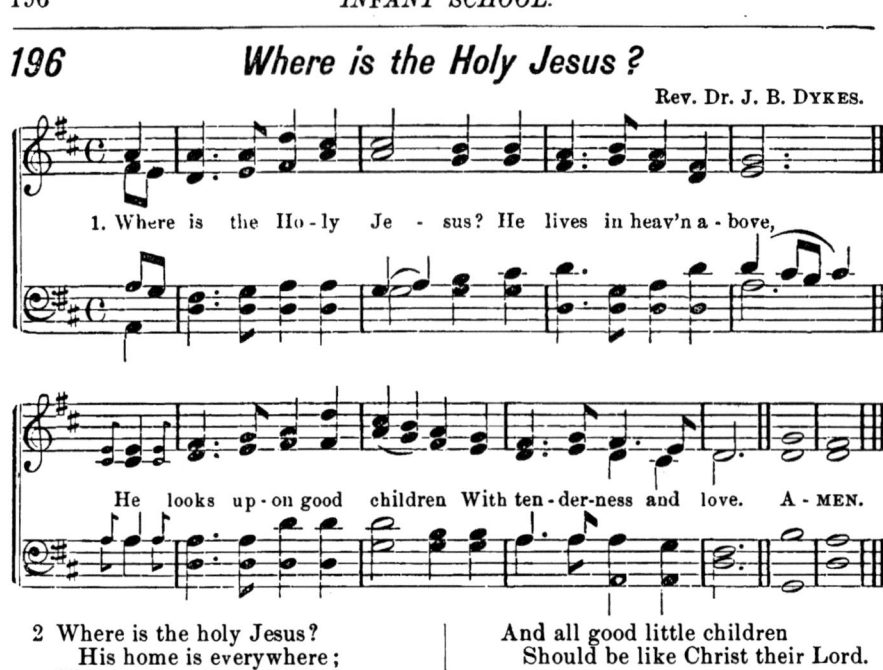

1. Where is the Holy Jesus? He lives in heav'n a - bove,
He looks up-on good children With ten-der-ness and love. A - MEN.

2 Where is the holy Jesus?
  His home is everywhere ;
He loves that little children
  Should speak to Him in prayer.

3 Once He came down from heaven
  And became a little child ;
He was so good and gentle,
  Obedient, meek, and mild,

4 He had no naughty tempers,
  He said no angry word,

And all good little children
  Should be like Christ their Lord.

5 For He will make them holy
  And teachable and mild,
And has sent His blessed Spirit
  To every Christian child.

6 Then, every night and morning
  When I kneel down to pray,
I will ask the holy Jesus
  To help me day by day. AMEN.

197   There is a Happy Land,

HAPPY LAND.

1. There is   a hap-py land, Far, far a - way, }
Where saints in glo-ry stand, Bright, bright as day. } Oh, how they sweetly sing,

HAPPY LAND.—Continued.

Worthy is the Saviour King, Loud let His praises ring, Praise, praise for aye! A - MEN.

2 Come to that happy land,
  Come, come away;
Why will ye doubting stand,
  Why still delay?
Oh we shall happy be
When, from sin and sorrow free,
Lord, we shall live with Thee,
  Blest, blest for aye.

3 Bright, in that happy land,
  Beams every eye;
Kept by a Father's hand
  Love cannot die.
Oh, then, to glory run,
Be a crown and kingdom won,
And, bright above the sun,
  We reign for aye.

198　Two Little Feet to Walk the Way to Heaven.

CORNISH MELODY.　　　　　　　　　　Arr. by A. NEVIN.

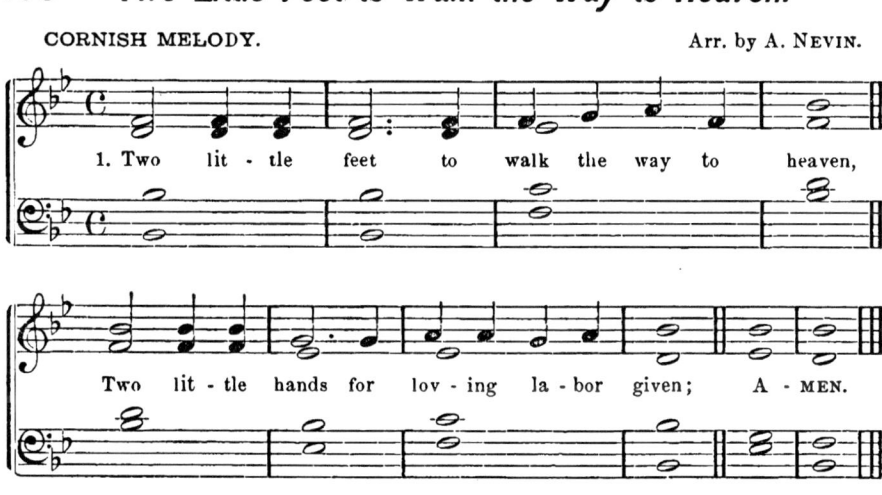

1. Two lit - tle feet to walk the way to heaven,

Two lit - tle hands for lov - ing la - bor given; A - MEN.

2 Two little eyes to read God's holy word,
  Two little lips to praise the blessed Lord;

3 One deathless soul, beaming with love and light,—
  So shall we live always in Jesus' sight. AMEN.

199   *Jesus Loves me, Jesus Loves me.*

MERTON.   Sac. Mus. Cabinet.

1. Je - sus loves me, Je - sus loves me, He is al - ways, al - ways near;

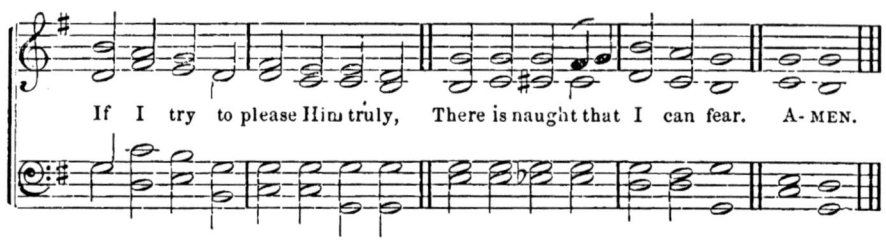

If I try to please Him truly, There is naught that I can fear. A- MEN.

2 Jesus loves me; well I know it,
    For to save my soul He died;
  He for me bore pain and sorrow,
    Nailèd hands and piercèd side.

3 Jesus loves me; night and morning
    Jesus hears the prayers I pray,
  And He never, never leaves me,
    When I work or when I play.

4 Jesus loves me, and He watches
    Over me with loving eye,
  And He sends His holy angels
    Safe to keep me till I die.

5 Jesus loves me; O Lord Jesu,
    Now I pray Thee by Thy love
  Keep me ever pure and holy
    Till I come to Thee above. AMEN.

200   *The Morning Bright.*

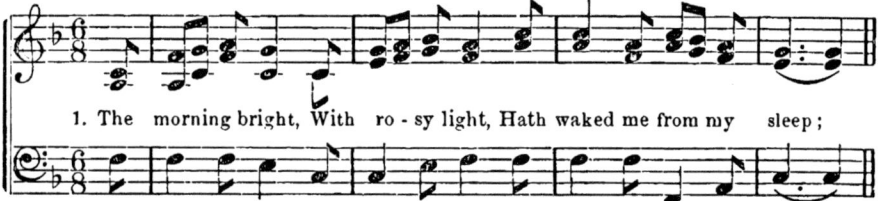

1. The morning bright, With ro - sy light, Hath waked me from my sleep;

THE MORNING BRIGHT.—Continued.

Fa-ther, I own Thy love a-lone Thy lit-tle one doth keep. A - MEN.

2 All through the day,
  I humbly pray,
Be Thou my Guard and Guide;
  My sins forgive,
  And let me live,
Blest Jesus, near Thy side.

3 Oh make Thy rest
  Within my breast,
Great Spirit of all grace;
  Make me like Thee,
  Then shall I be
Prepared to see Thy face. AMEN.

201 *Do no Sinful Action.*

A. NEVIN.

1. Do no sin - ful ac - tion, Speak no an - gry word;

We be - long to Je - sus, Chil - dren of the Lord. A - MEN.

2 Christ is kind and gentle,
  Christ is pure and true,
And His own dear children
  Must be holy too.

3 We are new-born Christians;
  We must learn to fight

With the bad within us,
  And to do the right.

4 Christ is our blest Master
  He is good and true,
And His own dear children
  Must be holy too. AMEN.

202   *I Think, when I Read that Sweet Story of Old.*

1. I think, when I read that sweet sto - ry of old, When

Je - sus was here a- mong men, How He called lit- tle chil- dren as

lambs to His fold, I should like to have been with Him then. A - MEN.

2 I wish that His hands had been placed on my head,
  That His arm had been thrown around me,
  And that I might have seen His kind look when He said,
  "Let the little ones come unto me."

3 Yet still to His footstool in prayer I may go,
  And ask for a share in His love ;

And if I thus earnestly seek Him below,
  I shall see Him and hear Him above,

4 In that beautiful place He has gone to prepare
  For all who are washed and forgiven,
  And many dear children are gathering there,
  "For of such is the kingdom of heaven." AMEN.

203 *When Little Samuel Woke.*

LENOX.　　　　　　　　　　　　　　　　　　　　J. EDSON.

1. When lit - tle Sam-uel woke, And heard his Maker's voice, At ev' - ry word He spoke How much did he re - joice! Oh bless - ed, hap - py child, to find The God of heav'n so near and kind, The God of heav'n so near and kind. A - MEN.

2 If God would speak to me,
　And say He was my Friend,
How happy I should be!
　Oh how I would attend l
The smallest sin I then would fear
If God almighty were so near.

And every sin I well may fear,
Since God almighty is so near.

8 And does He never speak?
　Oh yes, for in His word
He bids me come and seek
　The God that Samuel heard.

4 Like Samuel let me say,
　Whene'er I read His word,
"Speak, Lord; I would obey
　The voice that Samuel heard;"
And when I in Thy house appear,
"Speak, for Thy servant waits to
　hear." AMEN.

204　　　　　　　　*Jesus, Holy, Undefiled.*

Rev. Dr. J. B. DYKES.

1. Je - sus, ho - ly, un - de - filed, Lis - ten to a lit - tle child;

Thou hast sent the glo - rious light, Chas-ing far the si - lent night. A - MEN.

2 Thou hast sent the sun to shine
　O'er this glorious world of Thine,
　Warmth to give and pleasant glow
　On each tender flower below.

3 Now the little birds arise,
　Chirping gayly in the skies;
　Thee their tiny voices praise
　In the early songs they raise.

4 Thou by whom the birds are fed,
　Give to me my daily bread,
　And Thy Holy Spirit give,
　Without whom I cannot live.

5 Make me, Lord, in work and play,
　Thine more truly every day,
　And when Thou at last shall come,
　Take me to Thy heavenly home.

AMEN.

205　　　　　　　　*Glory to the Father give.*

ST. MARTINS.　　　　　　　　　　　　　　　Old French Melody.

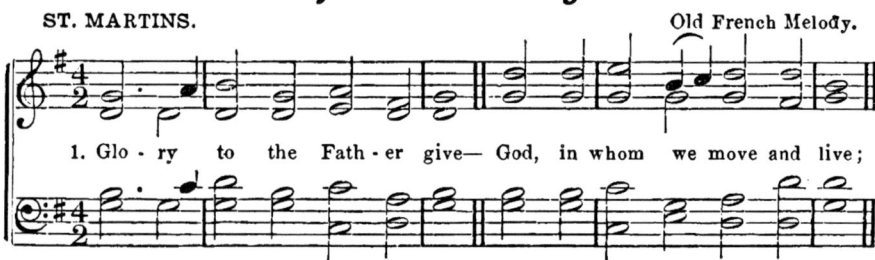

1. Glo - ry to the Fath - er give— God, in whom we move and live;

ST. MARTINS.—Continued.

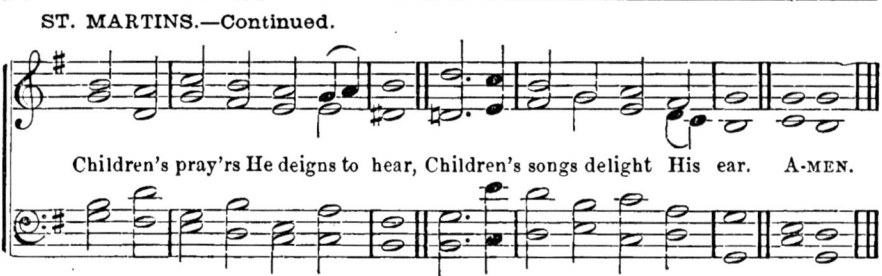

Children's pray'rs He deigns to hear, Children's songs delight His ear. A-MEN.

2 Glory to the Son we bring,
  Christ our Prophet, Priest, and King;
  Children, raise your sweetest strain
  To the Lamb, for He was slain.

3 Glory to the Holy Ghost,
  He reclaims the sinner lost;

Children's minds may He inspire,
Touch their tongues with holy fire.

4 Glory in the highest be
  To the blessed Trinity,
  For the gospel from above,
  For the word that "God is love." AMEN.

206   *Endless Praises to our Lord.*

GREGORIAN.

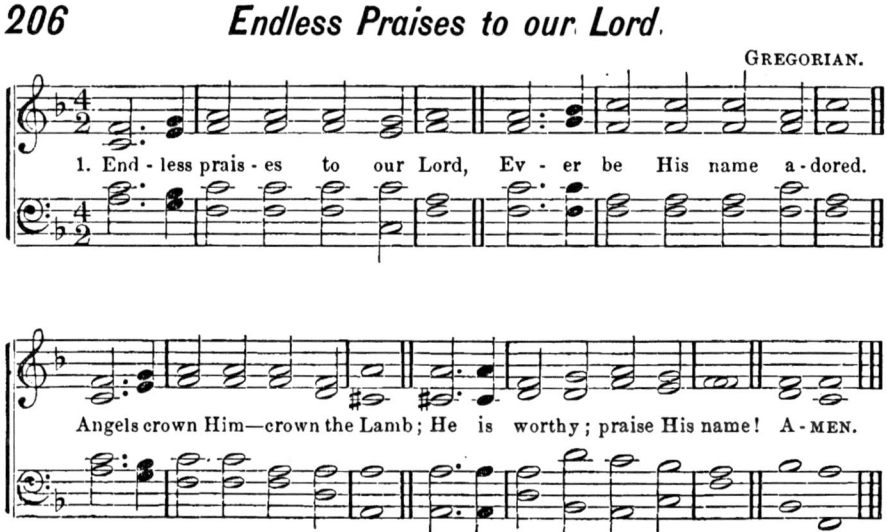

1. End - less prais - es   to   our Lord,   Ev - er   be   His   name   a - dored.

Angels crown Him—crown the Lamb; He   is   worthy; praise His name! A - MEN.

2 Now adore Him for His grace
  To our guilty, fallen race;
  Come, then, children, join to sing;
  "Glory to our God and King!" AMEN.

207 *I Love to Hear the Story.*

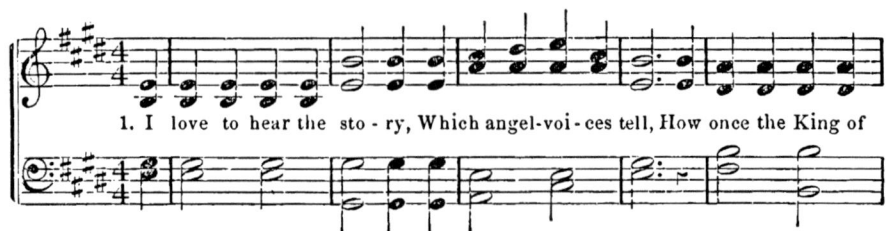

1. I love to hear the sto - ry, Which angel-voi - ces tell, How once the King of

glo - ry Came down on earth to dwell; I am both weak and sin - ful, But

this I surely know, The Lord came down to save me, Because He lov'd me so. AMEN.

2 I'm glad my blessed Saviour
   Was once a child like me,
 To show how pure and holy
   His little ones might be;
 And if I try to follow
   His footsteps here below,
 He never will forget me,
   Because He loves me so.

3 To sing His love and mercy
   My sweetest songs I'll raise;
 And though I cannot see Him,
   I know He hears my praise,
 For He has kindly promised
   That even I may go
 To sing among His angels,
   Because He loves me so.

208 *Once in Royal David's City.*

IRBY.   Dr. GAUNTLETT.

1. Once in roy - al Da - vid's cit - y Stood
Where a moth - er laid her Ba - by In a
low - ly cat - tle - shed, } Ma - ry was that moth - er mild,
man - ger for His bed; }
Je - sus Christ her lit - tle child. A - MEN.

2 He came down to earth from heaven
  Who is God and Lord of all,
And His shelter was a stable,
  And His cradle was a stall;
With the poor and mean and lowly
Lived on earth a Saviour holy.

3 And through all His wondrous child-
      hood
  He would honor and obey,
Love and watch the lowly maiden
  In whose gentle arms He lay;
Christian children all must be
Mild, obedient, good as He.

4 For He is our childhood's Pattern,
  Day by day like us He grew;
He was little, weak, and helpless,
  Tears and smiles like us He knew,
And He feeleth for our sadness,
And He shareth in our gladness.

5 And our eyes at last shall see Him,
  Through His own redeeming love,
For that Child so dear and gentle
  Is our Lord in heaven above,
And He leads His children on
To the place where He is gone.
                                          AMEN.

209   *Up Above the Bright Blue Sky.*

G. F. FLOWERS, Mus. Bac.

1. Up a - bove the bright blue sky, Where the stars are peep - ing,

Far - ther still than I can see, Heav'n - ly watch - ers

ov - er me Night - ly care are keep-ing. A - MEN.

2 And if, like the angels, I
  Could behold around me,
I should see them come and go,
Pass from heaven to earth below,
  And their hosts surround me.

3 All day long, and all night too,
  While I'm safely sleeping,
Busy on their task of love,
They are sent from heaven above,
  Faithful vigil keeping.

4 And whilst us from evil things
  Angels are defending,
Little children robed in white
Sing before the throne of light
  In daylight never ending.

5 Blessed Jesu, take me too,
  Though I'm weak and lowly ;
Let Thy gentle grace within
Make my garments white and clean,
  And my spirit holy. AMEN.

210   *There's a Friend for Little Children.*

ANON.

1. There's a Friend for lit - tle chil - dren A - bove the bright blue sky—

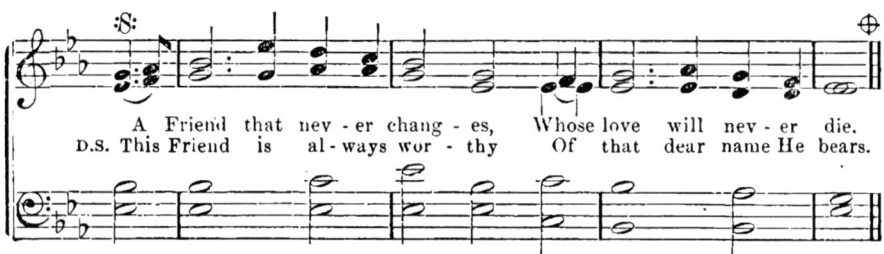

A Friend that nev - er chang - es, Whose love will nev - er die.

D.S. This Friend is al - ways wor - thy Of that dear name He bears.

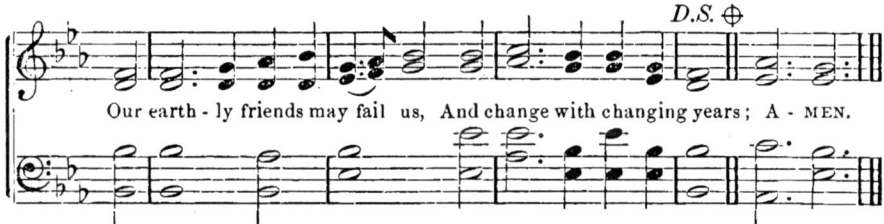

Our earth - ly friends may fail us, And change with changing years; A - MEN.

2 There's a home for little children
    Above the bright blue sky,
Where Jesus reigns in glory—
    A home of peace and joy;
No home on earth is like it,
    Nor can with it compare,
For every one is happy,
    Nor could be happier, there.

3 There's a crown for little children
    Above the bright blue sky,
And all who look for Jesus
    Shall wear it by and by—

A crown of brightest glory,
    Which He will then bestow
On those who found His favor
    And loved His name below.

4 There's a song for little children
    Above the bright blue sky,
And a harp of sweetest music
    And palms of victory.
All, all above is treasured,
    And found in Christ alone;
Lord, grant Thy little children
    To know Thee as their own. AMEN.

211   *Now the Day is Over.*

EVENING.   German.

1. Now the day is o - ver, Night is draw - ing nigh,

Shad-ows of the ev' - ning Steal a - cross the sky. A - MEN.

2 Now the darkness gathers,
  Stars begin to peep,
Birds and beasts and flowers
  Soon will be asleep.

3 Jesu, give the weary
  Calm and sweet repose;
With Thy tenderest blessing
  May our eyelids close.

4 Grant to little children
  Visions bright of Thee;
Guard the sailors tossing
  On the deep blue sea.

5 Comfort every sufferer
  Watching late in pain;
Those who plan some evil
  From their sin restrain.

6 Through the long night-watches
  May Thine angels spread
Their white wings above me,
  Watching round my bed.

7 When the morning wakens,
  Then may I arise
Pure and fresh and sinless
  In Thy holy eyes. AMEN.

212   *Jesus, like a Shepherd Tender.*

PRAISE.   8s & 7s.

1. Je - sus, like a shep-herd ten-der, Feeds His flock and gives them rest;

PRAISE.—Continued.

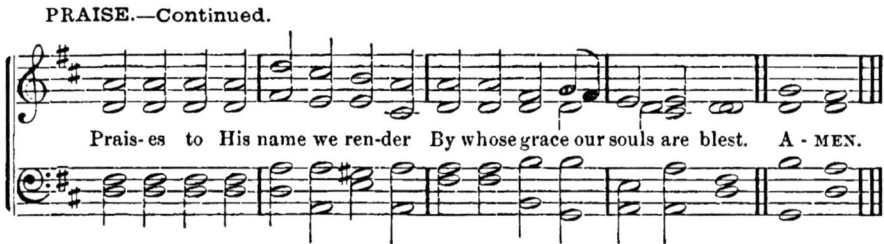

Prais-es to His name we ren-der By whose grace our souls are blest. A - MEN.

2 Feeble as we are, He careth
  For our wants from day to day;
Each His love and pity shareth,
  While He guides us in the way.

3 Holy Jesus, still direct us,
  While Thy lambs on earth are found;

Let Thy mighty power protect us
  As we pass where snares abound.

4 Keep us, save us, may we never
  Turn from Thee or grieve Thy love;
Feed us, lift us up for ever
  To Thy glorious fold above. AMEN.

213   *Jesus, Tender Shepherd.*

BERNHARD.   German.

1. Je - sus, ten-der Shepherd, hear me; Bless Thy lit - tle Lamb to - night;)
Through the darkness be Thou near me; Keep me safe till morning light. }

D.C. Through the darkness be Thou near me; Keep me safe till morning light.

Tender Shepherd, tender Shepherd, Keep me safe till morning light; A - MEN.

2 All this day Thy hand has led me,
  And I thank Thee for Thy care;
‖: Thou hast warmed me, clothed and fed me,
  Listen to my evening prayer. :‖
  Tender Shepherd, etc.

3 May my sins be all forgiven,
  Bless the friends I love so well;
‖: Take us, Lord, at last, to heaven,
  Happy there with Thee to dwell. :‖
  Tender Shepherd, etc.
  AMEN.

14

1   L. M.

PRAISE God, from whom all blessings flow,
Praise Him, all creatures here below;
Praise Him above, ye heavenly host,
Praise Father, Son, and Holy Ghost.
             AMEN.

2   8s.

To God the Father, God the Son,
And God the Spirit, Three in One,
Be glory in the highest given
By all in earth and all in heaven,
As was through ages heretofore,
Is now, and shall be evermore. AMEN.

3   C. M.

To Father, Son, and Holy Ghost,
   One God whom we adore,
Be glory as it was, is now,
   And shall be evermore. AMEN.

4   S. M.

To the eternal Three,
   In will and essence one,
To Father, Son, and Spirit be
   Coequal honors done. AMEN.

5   7s.

Sing we to our God above,
Praise eternal as His love;
Praise Him, all ye heavenly host,
Father, Son, and Holy Ghost.
             AMEN.

6   7s.

Praise the name of God most high,
Praise Him, all below the sky,
Praise Him, all ye heavenly host,
Father, Son, and Holy Ghost;
As through endless ages past,
Evermore His praise shall last. AMEN.

7   8s & 7s.

Lord, Thy glory fills the heaven,
   Earth is with its fullness stored;
Unto Thee be glory given,
   Holy, holy, holy Lord! AMEN.

8   8s, 7s, & 4.

Glory be to God the Father,
   Glory to th' eternal Son,
Sound aloud the Spirit's praises,
   Join the elders round the throne.
         Hallelujah,
Hail the glorious Three in One. AMEN.

9   7s & 6s.

Praise be to God the Father,
   Praise be to God the Son,
And praise to God the Spirit,
   The glorious Three in One;
With all the hosts of heaven
   We worship and adore
Thy triune name most holy,
   Now and for evermore. AMEN.

10   6s & 5s.

Glory to the Father,
   Glory to the Son,
And to Thee, blest Spirit,
   Whilst all ages run. AMEN.

11   H. M.

To God, the only wise,
   The one immortal King,
Let alleluias rise
   From ev'ry living thing;
Let earth and heaven, with all their host,
Praise Father, Son, and Holy Ghost.
             AMEN.

12   11s.

O Father almighty, to Thee be addressed,
With Christ and the Spirit, one God ever
       bless'd,
All glory and worship from earth and
       from heaven,
As was, and is now, and shall ever be
       given. AMEN.

INDEX OF HYMNS.

211

INFANT SCHOOL.

CAROLS.

INDEX OF CHANTS.

214

METRICAL INDEX.

First Presbyterian Church Sunday School

GERMANTOWN.

INTERMEDIATE DEPARTMENT.

ORDER OF WORSHIP.

9.12 FIRST BELL.   9.15 SECOND BELL.

PERFECT QUIET.

OPENING HYMN.

BIBLE DRILL.

PRAYER HYMN. (All to rise.)

PRAYER. (Repeated. All standing.)

BIBLE HYMN.

SHOW OF BIBLES BY TEACHERS AND SCHOLARS.

HYMN.

READING OF THE LESSON.

STUDY OF LESSON AND GOLDEN TEXT.

FIRST BELL:—Teachers will mark attendance, take up collection, etc.
SECOND BELL:—Quiet.
THIRD BELL:—Perfect Quiet.

HYMN.

LESSON.

HYMNS.

During the Singing the Books will be Distributed.

THE LORD'S PRAYER.

No. 1.

Uplift the banner! Let it float
Skyward and seaward, high and wide,
The sun shall light the shining folds,
The Cross on which the Saviour died.

Uplift the banner! Angels bend
In anxious silence o'er the sign,
And vainly seek to comprehend
The wonder of the love divine.   Amen.

Uplift the banner! Let it float
Skyward and seaward, high and wide,
Our glory only in the Cross,
Our only hope the Crucified.

Uplift the banner! Wide and high,
Skyward and seaward, let it shine;
Nor skill, nor might, nor merit ours;
We conquer only in that sign.   Amen.

No. 2.

We are but strangers here,
  Heav'n is our home;
Earth is a desert drear,
  Heav'n is our home.
Danger and sorrow stand
Round us on ev'ry hand,
Heav'n is our Fatherland,
  Heav'n is our home.

What though the tempests rage?
  Heav'n is our home;
Short is our pilgrimrge,
  Heav'n is our home.
And time's wild wintry blast
Soon shall be over-past,
We shall reach Home at last;
  Heav'n is our home.   Amen.

There at our Saviour's side,
  Heav'n is our home;
May we be glorified;
  Heav'n is our home.
There are the good and blest,
Those we love most and best,
Grant us with them to rest,
  Heav'n is our home.

Grant us to murmur not,
  Heav'n is our home;
Whate'er our earthly lot,
  Heav'n is our home.
Grant us at last to stand
There at Thine own right hand
Jesus, in Fatherland;
  Heav'n is our home.   Amen.

No. 3.

O Paradise! O Paradise!
  Who doth not crave for rest?
Who would not seek the happy land
  Where they that lov'd are blest?

Where loyal hearts and true
  Stand ever in the light,
All rapture thro' and thro',
  In God's most holy sight.   Amen.

O Paradise! O Paradise!
  The world is growing old;
Who would not be at rest and free
  Where love is never cold?

O Paradise! O Paradise!
  Wherefor doth death delay?
Bright death, that is the welcome dawn
  Of our eternal day;

O Paradise! O Paradise!
  The time will not be long.
Our souls already seem to hear
  Faint fragments of thy song;

Lord, Jesus, King of Paradise,
  O keep us in Thy love,
And guide us to that happy land
  Of perfect rest above.

No. 4.

O Jesus, Thou art standing
  Outside the fast-clos'd door;
In lowly patience waiting
  To pass the threshold o'er;
We bear the name of Christians,
  His Name and sign we bear;
O shame, thrice shame upon us,
  To keep Him standing there.   Amen.

O Jesus, Thou art knocking;
  And lo! that hand is scarr'd,
And thorns Thy brow encircle,
  And tears Thy face have marr'd.
O love that passeth knowledge,
  So patiently to wait!
O sin that hath no equal,
  So fast to bar the gate!

O Jesus Thou art pleading
  In accents meek and low,
"I died for you, my children,
  And will ye treat me so?"
O Lord with shame and sorrow
  We open now the door;
Dear Saviour, enter, enter,
  And leave us nevermore.   Amen.

No 5

"Forgive them, O My Father.
  They know not what they do!"
The Saviour spake in anguish
  As the sharp nails went through.

No pained reproaches gave He
  To them that shed His Blood,
But prayer and tenderest pity,
  Large as the love of God.

For me was that compassion,
  For me that tender care;
I need His wide forgiveness
  As much as any there.

It was my pride and hardness
  That hung Him on the tree;
Those cruel nails, O Saviour,
  Were driven in by me.

And often have I slighted
  Thy gentle Voice that chid;
Forgive me, too, Lord Jesus,
  I knew not what I did.

O Depth of sweet compassion!
  O Love Divine and True!
Save Thou the souls that slight Thee
  And know not what they do!   Amen.

No. 6.

Hushed was the evening hymn,
  The temple courts were dark;
The lamp was burning dim
  Before the sacred ark;
When suddenly a Voice Divine
Rang through the silence of the shrine.

The old man, meek and mild,
  The priest of Israel slept;
His watch the temple-child,
  The little Levite kept;
And what from Eli's sense was sealed,
The Lord to Hannah's son revealed.

O! give me Samuel's ear,
  The open ear, O Lord,
Alive and quick to hear
  Each whisper of Thy Word;
Like him to answer at Thy call,
And to obey Thee first of all.

O! give me Samuel's heart,
  A lowly heart, that waits
Where in Thy house Thou art,
  Or watches at Thy gates
By day and night; a heart that still
Moves at the breathing of Thy will.

O! give me Samuel's mind.
  A sweet unmurmuring faith,
Obedient and resigned
  To Thee in life and death;
That I may read with childlike eyes
Truths that are hidden from the wise.
                              Amen.

No. 7.

Angel voices ever singing
  Round Thy throne of light
Angel harps forever ringing,
  Rest not day nor night;
Thousands only live to bless Thee,
  And confess Thee,
    Lord of might!   Amen.

Thou, Who art beyond the farthest
  Mental eye can scan,
Can it be that Thou regardest
  Songs of sinful man?
Can we feel that Thou art near us,
  And wilt hear us?
    Yea, we can.

Yea, we know Thy love rejoices
  O'er each work of Thine;
Thou didst ears and hands and voices
  For Thy praise combine;
Craftman's art and music's measure
  For Thy pleasure
    Didst design.

Here, great God, to-day we offer
  Of Thine Own to Thee;
And for Thine acceptance proffer,
  All unworthily,
Hearts and minds, and hands and voices,
  In our choicest
    Melody.

Honor, glory, might and merit,
  Thine shall ever be,
Father, Son, and Holy Spirit,
  Blessed Trinity!
Of the best that Thou hast given
  Earth and Heaven
    Render Thee.   Amen.

No. 8.

Blessed Jesus, at Thy Word,
  We are gathered, all to hear Thee;
Let our hearts and souls be stirred,
  Now to seek and love and fear Thee.
By Thy teachings sweet and holy,
Drawn from earth to love Thee solely.

All our knowledge, sense, and sight,
  Lie in deepest darkness shrouded;
Till Thy Spirit breaks outright,
  With the beams of truth unclouded.
Thou alone to God can'st win us,
Thou must work all good within us.

Glorious Lord, Thyself impart
  Light of light from God proceeding,
Open Thou our eyes and heart,
  Help us by Thy Spirit's pleading.
Hear the cry Thy people raises,
Hear, and bless our prayers and praises.
                  Amen.

No. 9.

Jesus, meek and gentle,
  Son of God most high,
Pitying, loving Saviour,
  Hear Thy children's cry.

Give us holy freedom,
  Fill our hearts with love;
Draw us, Holy Jesus,
  To the realms above.

Lead us on our journey,
  Be, Thyself. the way
Through terrestrial darkness,
  To celestial day.

Jesus, meek and gentle,
  Son of God most high,
Pitying, loving Saviour,
  Hear Thy children's cry.

No. 10.

Ever would I fain be reading
  In the ancient Holy Book,
Of my Saviour's gentle pleading,
  Truth in every word and look.

How when children came, He blessed them,
  Suffered no man to reprove;
Took them in His arms and pressed them
  To His heart with words of love.

How no contrite soul e'er sought Him,
  And was bidden to depart;
How with gentle words he taught him,
  Took the death from out his heart.

Still I read the ancient story,
  And my joy is ever new;
How for us He left His glory,
  How He still is kind and true.

No. 11.

Humble praises, holy Jesus,
  Infant voices raise to Thee.
In Thy mercy, oh! receive us,
  Suffer us Thy lambs to be.

  Halleluia, sweetly singing,
    Joyful tribute now we bring;
  Halleluia, halleluia,
    Halleluia to our King.

Gracious Saviour, be Thou with us,
  Let Thy mercy richly flow;
Let Thy Spirit, blessed Jesus,
  Light and life on us bestow.

No. 12.

Saviour, blessed Saviour,
  Listen while we sing,
Hearts and voices raising
  Praises to our King.
All we have to offer,
  All we hope to be,
Body. soul, and spirit
  All we yield to Thee.

Nearer, ever nearer,
  Christ we draw to Thee;
Deep in adoration,
  Bending low the knee.
Thou for our redemption
  Cam'st on earth to die;
Thou, that we might follow,
  Hast gone up on high.

No. 13.

Glory be to God the Father!
  Glory be to God the Son!
Glory be to God the Spirit!
  Great Jehovah, three in one!

  Glory! Glory!
  While eternal ages run!
  Glory! Glory!
  While eternal ages run!

Glory be to Him that loved us,
  Washed us from each spot and stain;
Glory be to Him who bought us,
  Made us kings with Him to reign.

No. 14.

To God be the glory! great things He hath
  done:
So loved He the world that He gave us His
  Son;
Who yielded His life an atonement for sin,
And opened the Life-gate that all may go in.

  Praise the Lord! praise the Lord!
    Let the earth hear His voice!
  Praise the Lord! praise the Lord!
    Let the people rejoice!
  Oh, come to the Father thro' Jesus the
    Son;
  And give Him the glory! great things He
    hath done!

O perfect redemption, the purchase of
  blood,
To ev'ry believer the promise of God;
The vilest offender who truly believes,
That moment from Jesus a pardon receives.

Great things He hath taught us, great
  things He hath done,
And great our rejoicing thro' Jesus the Son;
But purer, and higher, and greater will be
Our wonder, our transport, when Jesus we
  see.

No. 15.

More about Jesus would I know,
More of His grace to others show;
More of His saving fullness see,
More of His love who died for me.

  More, more about Jesus,
  More, more about Jesus;
  More of His saving fullness see;
  More of His love, who died for me.

More about Jesus let me learn,
More of His holy will discern;
Spirit of God, my teacher be,
Showing the things of Christ to me.

More about Jesus; in His word,
Holding communion with my Lord;
Hearing His voice in every line,
Making each faithful saying mine.

More about Jesus; on His throne,
Riches in glory all His own;
More of His kingdom's sure increase;
More of His coming, Prince of Peace.

No. 16.

Sitting at the feet of Jesus,
  O what words I hear Him say!
Happy place! so near, so precious!
  May it find me there each day:
Sitting at the feet of Jesus,
  I would look upon the past;
For His love has been so gracious,
  It has won my heart at last.

Sitting at the feet of Jesus,
  Where can mortal be more blest?
There I lay my sins and sorrows,
  And, when weary, find sweet rest:
Sitting at the feet of Jesus,
  There I love to weep and pray,
While I from His fullness gather
  Grace and comfort ev'ry day.

Bless me, O my Saviour, bless me,
  As I sit low at Thy feet;
Oh, look down in love upon me,
  Let me see Thy face so sweet,
Give me, Lord, the mind of Jesus,
  Make me holy as He is;
May I prove I've been with Jesus,
  Who is all my righteousness.

No. 17.

Are you weary, are you heavy hearted?
  Tell it to Jesus, tell it to Jesus.
Are you grieving over joys departed?
  Tell it to Jesus alone.

Tell it to Jesus, tell it to Jesus,
  He is a friend that's well known;
You have no other such a friend or brother;
  Tell it to Jesus alone.

Do the tears flow down your cheeks un-
  bidden?
  Tell it to Jesus, tell it to Jesus.
Have you sins that to man's eyes are hid-
  den?
  Tell it to Jesus alone.

Do you fear the gath'ring clouds of sorrow?
  Tell it to Jesus, tell it to Jesus.
Are you anxious what shall be to-morrow?
  Tell it to Jesus alone.

Are you troubled at the thought of dying?
  Tell it to Jesus, tell it to Jesus.
For Christ's coming Kingdom are you sigh-
  ing?
  Tell it to Jesus alone.

No. 18.

Gentle Jesus, meek and mild,
Look upon a little child;
Pity my simplicity;
Suffer me to come to Thee.   Amen.

Lamb of God I look to Thee,
Thou shalt my Example be:
Thou art gentle, meek and mild,
Thou wast once a little Child.

Loving Jesus, gentle Lamb,
In Thy gracious Hands I am;
Make me, Saviour, what Thou art,
Live Thyself within my heart.

I shall then show forth Thy praise,
Serve Thee all my happy days;
Then the world shall always see
Christ, the Holy Child, in me.   Amen.

No. 19.

Arise and hail the Sacred Day,
Cast all low cares of life away;
And thoughts of meaner things;
This day, to cure our deadly woes,
The Sun of Righteousness arose
   With healing in His wings.   Amen.

How wonderful, how vast His love,
Who left the shining realms above,
   Those happy seats of rest;
How much for lost mankind He bore,
Their peace and pardon to restore,
   Can never be expressed.

While we adore His boundless grace,
And pious joy and mirth take place
   Of sorrow, grief and pain,
Give glory to our God on high,
And not, among the general joy,
   Forget good-will to men.

O then let Heaven and earth rejoice,
Creation's whole united voice,
   And hymn the Sacred Day,
When sin and Satan vanquished fell,
And all the powers of death and hell,
   Before His sovereign sway.   Amen.

No. 20.

Once in royal David's city
   Stood a lowly cattle-shed,
Where a mother laid her Baby
   In a manger for His bed;
Mary was that mother mild,
Jesus Christ her little Child.   Amen.

He came down to earth from heaven,
   Who is God and Lord of all,
And His shelter was a stable,
   And His cradle was a stall:
With the poor, and mean, and lowly,
Lived on earth our Saviour Holy.

And our eyes at last shall see Him,
   Through His own redeeming love,
For that Child so dear and gentle
   Is our Lord in Heaven above;
And He leads His children on
To the place where He is gone.

Not in that poor lowly stable,
   With the oxen standing by,
We shall see Him; but in Heaven,
   Set at God's Right Hand on high;
When like stars His children crowned
All in white shall wait around.   Amen.

No. 21.

Ten thousand times ten thousand
   In sparkling raiment bright,
The armies of the ransomed saint
   Throng up the steeps of light:
'Tis finished, all is finished,
   Their fight with death and sin;
Fling open wide the golden gates,
   And let the victors in.   Amen.

What rush of alleluias
   Fills all the earth and sky;
What ringing of a thousand harps
   Bespeaks the triumph nigh.
O day, for which Creation
   And all its tribes were made;
O joy, for all its former woes
   A thousand fold repaid.

O then what raptured greetings
   On Canaan's happy shore;
What knitting severed friendships up,
   Where partings are no more.
Then eyes with joy shall sparkle,
   That brimmed with tears of late;
Orphans no longer fatherless,
   Nor widows desolate.

Bring near Thy great salvation,
   Thou Lamb for sinners slain!
Fill up the roll of Thine elect,
   Then take Thy power, and reign!
Appear, Desire of Nations,
   Thine exiles long for home!
Show in the heaven Thy promised sign;
   Thou Prince and Saviour come!   Amen.

No. 22.

Light after darkness, gain after loss,
Strength after weakness, crown after cross;
Sweet after bitter, hope after fears,
Home after wand'ring, praise after tears.

Sheaves after sowing, sun after rain,
Sight after mystery, peace after pain;
Joy after sorrow, calm after blast,
Rest after weariness, sweet rest at last.

Near after distant, gleam after gloom,
Love after loneliness, life after tomb;
After long agony, rapture of bliss,
Right was the pathway, leading to this.

No. 23.

The King of love my Shepherd is,
  Whose goodness faileth never:
I nothing lack if I am His
  And He is mine forever.   Amen.

Where streams of living water flow
  My ransomed soul He leadeth,
And, where the verdant pastures grow,
  With food celestial feedeth.

In death's dark vale I fear no ill
  With Thee, dear Lord, beside me;
Thy rod and staff my comfort still,
  Thy Cross before to guide me.

And so through all the length of days
  Thy goodness faileth never;
Good Shepherd may I sing Thy praise
  Within Thy house forever.   Amen.

No. 24.

Jesus, my Lord, to Thee I cry,
Unless Thou help me, I must die;
Oh, bring Thy free salvation nigh,
  And take me as I am.

    Take me as I am,
    Take me as I am;
    Lord, I give myself to Thee,
    Oh, take me as I am.

Helpless I am and full of guilt,
But yet for me Thy blood was spilt;
And Thou canst make me what Thou wilt,
  And take me as I am.

I bow before Thy mercy-seat,
Behold me, Saviour, at Thy feet;
Thy work begin, Thy work complete,
  And take me as I am.

If Thou hast work for me to do,
Inspire my will, my heart renew;
And work both in, and by me too,
  And take me as I am.

And when at last the work is done,
The battle fought, the victory won;
Still, still my cry shall be alone,
  Oh, take me as I am.

No. 25.

Every morning the red sun
  Rises warm and bright;
But the evening cometh on,
  And the dark, cold night;
There's a bright Land far away,
Where is never ending day.   Amen.

Every spring the sweet young flowers
  Open bright and gay,
Till the chilly autumn hours
  Wither them away:
There's a Land we have not seen,
Where the trees are always green.

Christ our Lord is ever near
  Those who follow Him!
But we cannot see Him here,
  For our eyes are dim;
There is a most happy Place,
Where men always see His Face.

Who shall go to that bright Land?
  All who do the right;
Holy children there shall stand
  In their robes of white;
For that Heaven so bright and blest
Is our everlasting Rest.   Amen.

No. 26.

Child Jesus came to earth one day,
  To save us sinners dying;
And cradled in the straw and hay,
  The Holy One was lying.
The Star shone down the Child to greet,
The lowing oxen near His feet.
  Alleluia! Alleluia, Child Jesus!

Take courage, soul so weak and worn,
  Thy sorrows have departed;
A Child in David's town was born,
  To heal the broken-hearted.
Then let us haste this Child to find
And children be in heart and mind.
  Alleluia! Alleluia, Child Jesus!   Amen.

No. 27.

We come in the might of the Lord of Light,
In singing train to meet Him;
And we put to flight the armies of night,
That the sons of the day may greet Him.

We march, we march to victory!
With the Cross of the Lord before us,
With His loving Eye looking down from
the sky,
And His Holy Arms spread o'er us.

Our sword is the Spirit of God on high,
Our helmet is His salvation,
Our banner the Cross of Calvary,
Our watchword—The Incarnation.

And the choir of angels with songs awaits
Our march to the Golden Sion;
For our Captain has broken the brazen
gates,
And burst the bars of iron.

No. 28.

Forward! be our watchword,
Steps and voices join'd;
Seek the things before us,
Not a look behind:
Burns the fiery pillar
At our army's head;
Who shall dream of shrinking,
By our Captain led?
Forward thro' the desert,
Thro' the toil and fight:
Jordan flows before us.
Sion beams with light!

Glories upon glories,
Hath our God prepared,
By the souls that love Him
One day to be shar'd;
Eye hath not beheld them,
Ear hath never heard;
Nor of these hath utter'd
Tho't or speech a word:
Forward, marching forward
Where the heav'n is bright,
Till the veil be lifted.
Till our faith be sight.   Amen.

To th' Eternal Father
Loudest anthems raise;
To the Son and Spirit
Echo songs of praise:

To the Lord of Glory,
Blessed Three in One,
Be by men and angels
Endless honor done.
Weak are earthly praises,
Dull the songs of night;
Forward into triumph,
Forward into Light!   Amen.

No. 29.

Praise, O praise the King of Heaven,
To His feet your tribute bring;
Ransom'd, heal'd, restor'd, forgiven,
Evermore His praises sing;
Alleluia! Alleluia!
Praise the everlasting King!

Praise Him for His grace and favor
To our fathers in distress;
Praise Him, still the same as ever,
Slow to chide and swift to bless;
Alleluia! Alleluia!
Glorious in His faithfulness.

Father-like, He tends and spares us,
Well our feeble frame He knows;
In His hands He gently bears us,
Rescues us from all our foes;
Alleluia! Alleluia!
Widely yet His mercy flows

Angels in the height adore Him!
Ye behold Him face to face;
Saints triumphant bow before Him,
Gather'd in from ev'ry race.
Alleluia! Alleluia!
Praise with us the God of grace.   Amen.

No. 30.

Alleluia! Song of gladness,
Song of everlasting joy;
Alleluia! Song the sweetest
That can angel hosts employ.
Alleluia! Church victorious,
Thou may'st lift this joyful strain;
Alleluia! songs of triumph
Well befit the ransom'd train.

Alleluia! Let our voices
Rise to heav'n in full accord;
Alleluia! ev'ry moment
Brings us nearer to the Lord.
But our earnest supplication
Holy God, we raise to Thee;
Brings us to Thy blissful presence,
Let us all Thy glory see.   Amen.

THE COMMANDMENTS—(To be read responsively, by Superintendent and School.)

I.
Thou shalt have no other gods before me.

II.
Thou shalt not make unto thee any graven image, or any likeness of any thing that is in heaven above, or that is in the earth beneath, or that is in the water under the earth: thou shalt not bow down thyself to them, nor serve them: for I the Lord thy God am a jealous God, visiting the iniquity of the fathers upon the children unto the third and fourth generation of them that hate me: and shewing mercy unto thousands of them that love me, and keep my commandments.

III.
Thou shalt not take the name of the Lord thy God in vain · for the Lord will not hold him guiltless that taketh his name in vain.

IV.
Remember the sabbath day to keep it holy. Six days shalt thou labor, and do all thy work: but the seventh day is the sabbath of the Lord thy God; in it thou shalt not do any work, thou, nor thy son, nor thy daughter, thy manservant, nor thy maidservant, nor thy cattle, nor thy stranger that is within thy gates: for in six days the Lord made heaven and earth, the sea, and all that in th and rested the seventh day; wherefore the Lord t the sabbath day, and hallowed it.

V.
Honor thy father and thy mother; that thy days long upon the land which the Lord thy God giveth t

VI.
Thou shalt not kill.

VII.
Thou shalt not commit adultery.

VIII.
Thou shalt not steal.

IX.
Thou shalt not bear false witness against thy neigl

X.
Thou shalt not covet thy neighbor's house, thou not covet thy neighbor's wife, nor his manservant, i maidservant, nor his ox, nor his ass, nor any thing thy neighbor's.

HYMN.

SHOW OF BIBLES BY TEACHERS AND SCHOLARS.

QUESTIONS TO BE ANSWERED BY THE SCHOOL:
WHAT IS THE TITLE OF THE LESSON OF THE DAY?
WHAT IS THE GOLDEN TEXT?
GIVE THE BOOK, CHAPTER, VERSES OF THE LESSON.

RESPONSIVE SCRIPTURE READING OF THE LESSON.

MISSIONARY OFFERINGS IN CLASSES AND ATTENDANCE CARDS TO BE MARKED.

BIBLE STUDY IN CLASSES.

BELL SIGNAL—(Lesson Study to close).

SINGING—(New Hymn).

NOTICES

SINGING. (If time permits.)

SUPERINTENDENT'S CLOSING WORDS.

SUPERINTENDENT WILL ANNOUNCE ATTENDANCE and the amount of the collection, and classes all present.

CLOSING HYMN.

LORD'S PRAYER—(In unison) to be followed by text, repeated by all.
Our Father which art in heaven, hallowed be thy name. Thy kingdom come. Thy will be done in as it is in heaven: give us this day our daily bread; and forgive us our debts as we forgive our debtors. An us not into temptation, but deliver us from evil. For thine is the kingdom, and the power, and the gl01 ever. Amen.

The Lord watch between me and thee when we are absent one from anothe
—Gen. xx

DISMISSION.

CPSIA information can be obtained at www.ICGtesting.com
Printed in the USA
BVOW05s1041031215

429265BV00027B/552/P